WORK IT OUT

TRIGGER™
The mental health & wellbeing publisher

WORK IT OUT

I loved it. A brilliant and frank look at something that absolutely needs to be talked about in this way. A grippingly honest account that so many of us are silently experiencing. Reading Fiona's honest and human account of how to cope in the modern world is only going to be good for your mental health.
Jo Love, lobellaloves.com

A refreshingly honest account of the highs and lows of social media and mental health.
Mikhila McDaid, blogger and content creator

ABOUT THE AUTHOR

Fiona Thomas is from South Lanarkshire, UK, and was diagnosed with depression in 2012. She was unable to work for almost a year, and turned to blogging in that time as a hobby. However, though it started off as a way to pass time, Fiona quickly became obsessed with the online world, leading her to experience high levels of anxiety.

Now a proud advocate for technology as a communication tool for those of us who suffer the crippling symptoms of mental illness, Fiona has used the internet to help hone her identity and create a supportive community.

Fiona is a freelance writer with work published on *Metro, Healthline, Heads Together, Mind, Reader's Digest*, and *Happiful* magazine. She also facilitates creative writing workshops and offers private mentoring. This book is an extension of her work, and a celebration of all that's possible through the power of social media. Her second book *Out of Office: Ditch the 9-5 and Be Your Own Boss* is a guide to freelancing and was shortlisted for a Business Book Award.

ABOUT THE AUTHOR

WORK IT OUT

Finding Connection in the Digital Age without Falling Apart

Fiona Thomas

TRIGGER™

The mental health & wellbeing publisher

This edition published in 2023 by Trigger Publishing
An imprint of Shaw Callaghan Ltd

UK Office
The Stanley Building
7 Pancras Square
Kings Cross
London N1C 4AG

US Office
On Point Executive Center, Inc
3030 N Rocky Point Drive W
Suite 150
Tampa, FL 33607
www.triggerhub.org

A CIP catalogue record for this book is available upon request from
the British Library
ISBN: 978-1-83796-393-5
Ebook ISBN: 978-1-83796-394-2

For Lucy and Poppy

CONTENTS

PROLOGUE

It's 2012 and I'm pretending to be a functioning adult.

"The glitter on the bathroom floor is pretty," I think. Considering I've been making a habit of staring at this spot for the past six months instead of doing my actual job, I'm surprised I haven't seen it before.

Why hadn't I noticed it before?

Reaching down for the sparkles it's clear that they are part of the rubber flooring which is covered in years of scuff marks from the catering staff trailing in and out. The glitter has always been there.

I look up at the ceiling. Is that a new bulb? It's blinding. Scrunching my eyes for a moment of relief, I lean on the partition which divides my current space from the one next to me and take a couple of deep breaths.

I'm safe in the bathroom.

Laughter echoes down the concrete hallway outside and I pull my knees up and hug them in for protection. Two people are talking about going to a knitting class this evening and it makes me inexplicably angry, knowing that they have hobbies and happiness. I try to out-think the pain, sucking in air like I've seen them do in films.

Three hours I spent zoned out this morning, staring at the wall in my office which is painted the most horrific shade of yellow. No one had noticed. I'm glad of that.

This particular day – the day when the floor glitter and the lightbulb make me feel attacked – nothing in particular has happened. There hasn't been an argument with the chef, even though he hates me so much that I swear he'd chop me up and put me in the daily special within a heartbeat if he could. There's no staff appraisal where I have to repeat standards and policies to a team of friendly faces who are trying their best to earn a living and have a good time. The sound of my own voice bores and terrifies me in equal measure.

A few weeks ago, I did a stock take that involved counting thousands of individual items. It took two full days and as I was inputting the data into the computer I accidentally deleted everything. The following day at 5am, alone, I started to recount from scratch. There were tears on the bus home that night.

I can no longer be near my carefree, fresh-faced staff members, whose frivolous activities, like meeting for after-work drinks, send me spiralling into a silent rage. It feels like I'm being punished. Not by them, of course – they all kindly invite me out to socialize every time and I always decline – but by my life choices which seem to have forced me right into the role of "responsible adult" without much room for anything else. Except guilt, there's always room for guilt.

I watch them get changed at the end of a shift, putting on makeup, and brushing their hair while I quietly tap numbers into a spreadsheet, resentment brewing, trying to ignore them. I can't help but think back to the person I used to be just a few years ago. I went to gigs, started bands with my mates, worked on fun projects like homemade zines, and stayed up until sunrise watching the final episode of *Lost*.

But I had my chance at fun.

Studying music at university was my opportunity to have a creative life and I didn't take it. Instead, I took what I thought was the easier option. A promotion in my café job, a foot on the ladder. My choices led me here and I have to deal with the consequences. What's the alternative? Normally I can shake off the dark thoughts that are lingering. Not today.

I cry for a few minutes and try to regain my composure, but how much composure can you find when you're hiding in a toilet? I try to stand up and exit the cubicle to go back to my office, but I can't seem to move.

Like I said, there's no direct reason for today's breakdown, so the plan is – if you can even call it a plan at all – to have a private little crisis in my own time and then get on with the day as though nothing has happened.

Because nothing *has* happened.

That's what I've been doing for the last few weeks (or has it been longer?) and it's been working out just fine, so I have no reason to believe that it won't continue to be an effective way of dealing with my problems.

But today, I just can't seem to execute a crucial part of the plan.

I can't leave my favourite bathroom stall.

My body just doesn't want me to go back to work.

It's funny because right up until this moment, I had never seen a way out. I'd always thought that there's no other direction other than forward, no answer other than yes, and no choice but to carry on. I've always done what has been expected of me, no matter how difficult it might be or how sick it makes me feel. Conformity always wins.

But on this day, for some reason, another option rears its head. The choice to do nothing. I could stop pretending that I am OK. I could stop pretending that I am dealing with everything just fine. I could just stop.

It feels like my body is going through an emergency shutdown, the mental equivalent of pulling the fire alarm to get out of an exam, to run.

I'm closing for business.

I stay in the bathroom stall for a while longer, reaching for my phone. I press down on the button at the top, bringing life to the screen, pull up the browser, and start to type:

"What are the symptoms of depression?"

INTRODUCTION

Asking for help is not failing. It's winning on so many levels.

But, of course, that's not what I thought, over a decade ago, when I was sifting through the internet looking for mental health support. I'm going to assume that you've picked up this book because you are anticipating, have already experienced, or are in the middle of a difficult period in your life. You might be switching yourself off mentally in order to cope with your day-to-day activities, or maybe you feel an unexplained state of fear, dread or hopelessness. To sum up, you probably feel a bit disconnected.

Which is weird, right? We live in a hyperconnected world where we can video call with family a thousand miles away, watch movies on our phones, share selfies with thousands of followers, settle arguments with one swift Google search and snoop on our enemies 24/7. The joy of connection is electrifying, addictive.

From the outside it might look like you have it all. A great family, relationship, home and career. But is there an unsettling disconnect between how things appear and how things feel on the inside? Does your existence feel off-balance? Are your emotions unstable? Is your sense of belonging swinging on a pendulum from one extreme to another?

If disconnection is the ailment, I believe that working on your ability to connect can be the treatment. Connection is the key to unlocking purpose, the secret sauce for a more fulfilling existence, the path to a bright and meaningful future.

What do you really want your life to look like?

Does having a career feel like an absolute must for you? Are you unemployed and wondering how you fit into society without a job? Perhaps you're stuck in a job you hate, or feel indifferent about, and want to know if it's worth seeking something more exciting. Or maybe you don't have a clue what you want, maybe you're just aware of a feeling brewing in your gut, a need for something more, a solution to a feeling of detachment, of being not quite where you need to be, of being not quite here at all. If you're looking for direction, connection and purpose, then this book is for you.

We now have more choice than ever, with the ability to learn new skills from YouTube tutorials and online courses, the chance to apply for and work in roles thousands of miles away, not to mention the curbside view of how others live their lives, both strangers and friends. We can side hustle from our bedrooms and work in different time zones, and while this has been somewhat true for many years, the lockdowns that we experienced during the COVID-19 pandemic heightened the need for everyone to take part in the online version of connection. Whether using the internet for work, social reasons, hobbies or to upskill, it's fair to say that the world is your oyster.

But finding those pearls of wisdom is hard to master. To beat the paralysis that comes with a world of possibilities you must strengthen, above all else, the bond you have with yourself. Without that sense of connection with what you truly want, you might lose yourself in what you think you *should* be doing, what you think your *parents* want, what *brands* or *influencers* tell you to want, and what you think would *look good* to others. Knowing who you are at your core will have a ripple effect, helping you feel more connected to the world around you and those in it.

At the beginning of 2020 I was putting the finishing touches to my book about freelancing, *Out of Office: Ditch the 9–5 and Be Your Own Boss*. My mission was to show my readers that getting out of the traditional office environment and taking control of their schedule could transform their working lives and give them the tools to build a thriving business. By the time the paperback was published, the vast majority of the world had been working from home in some capacity for over seven months.

Insomnia was a common occurrence for me during those stressful months, so in the early hours one morning as my husband at the time, Joe, slept next to me, I did what felt like second nature; I opened Instagram. There was a message from a woman called Diane, a long, rambling burst of vulnerability from a person I'd never met, one that could be summed up in one sentence. Digitally, Diane whispered: "What am I doing with my life?"

As a result of the global pandemic, industries have been forced to figure out remote working models, allowing people to work from home wherever possible. Lots of companies saw a rise in productivity and a fall in expenditure; as a result, hybrid working has become the norm, with as many as 70 per cent of workers saying they would prefer to work anywhere, anytime and value this over a promotion. On the flip-side, some workers have been hit hard by losing connections with colleagues, distractions at home, and increased difficulty communicating and collaborating.

During those long days of lockdown, I helped freelancers pivot into new markets and spoke on the radio about why self-employment was still a financially secure career option. Podcast hosts asked me if I was glad to be working for myself and time and time again, I said yes. Although working for myself is helping me create the life I desire, it's not the catch-all solution for people who feel unfulfilled. During the global pause when so many people were questioning where to turn and how to pursue their dreams, I was in a privileged position to be confident in my career path. A few steps ahead of people like Diane, I had life experience that I could share with others to help them find a way through the messy middle.

For that reason, I had the idea to revisit this book and make some radical changes to both its form and content. A perfectionist at heart, I have removed some parts and rewritten over a hundred new pages to offer prompts and solutions that will help you nurture a stronger connection with yourself and the world around you.

About this book

First and foremost, this book is a memoir designed to be read from start to finish. A collection of moments from my life that show me as a young adult trying to work out how to live life, build a career, fit in socially, survive mental illness and start afresh. At the beginning of each section, I've added a short introduction to explain why I'm sharing my story and what you can gain from reading it. Seeing yourself in a story can be a comfort in times of need, a nudge in the right direction when you're ready to make a move, a pep talk to push forward.

I've added in more practical elements to help you work out how to apply my experience to your own set of circumstances. Unlike me, you may not have unfulfilled childhood dreams of being a pop star, but you probably had idols who at one point made you feel seen in the wider world. You may never have been promoted to the catering manager of a busy tourist attraction, but you've probably felt a similar pressure to do work that feels at odds with who you are as a person. You may never have bared your soul on the internet, but you've probably craved a deeper emotional connection with the people around you.

Everyone has a breaking point, something that has the potential to make you re-evaluate how you see the world and how you spend your time. Although my story centres around my breakdown and the resulting isolation and stigma around depression and anxiety, it's my hope that you can see yourself on the pages too. That you can avoid a breaking point or if not, at least use it as the catalyst for a brighter future. Here's what I want for you:

- A connection with your own sense of meaning.
- A connection to things that bring you joy.
- A connection to the people who matter most to you.
- A connection to your community.

- A connection to your emotions.
- A connection to your inner strength
  and resilience.

It took a mental breakdown for me to realize that my life was not reflective of what I actually wanted. Whether it's a health crisis, the ending of a relationship, the loss of a loved one, unexpected redundancy or a global pandemic ... These things can shake your foundations and give you the option to rebuild. You may not know what that looks like just yet, and that's OK. But let me tell you that my breaking point was the most painful and powerful moment of my life. Now, I work on my own terms, writing books and facilitating spaces for other writers. Every day I wake up at a time that suits me, I have the flexibility to work from a café, on the beach or in bed, and I've honed a network of freelancers who I meet online a few times a week. Many of my clients have become close friends and they are a pleasure to interact with. My earning potential has no ceiling, I can afford therapy, city breaks and medication to maintain my mental health. I'm connected to the work I do and the people I surround myself with. Life is good.

This book is about navigating your version of this process while maintaining a connection to the things that matter to you.

How to use this book

There is no foolproof method or strategy that I can teach you, but I can offer you a mindset shift, a different way of thinking that will open your eyes to the possibilities around you and the potential within yourself. A way to move away from feeling lost to feeling connected at your core with yourself and the world.

When finding your bearings in life, it's important to anchor yourself in the here and now before you take any major steps. But how do you figure out where you are? Journaling is the perfect tool for gaining mental clarity amidst the overwhelming nature of modern life. Journaling with pen and paper is physical, so it connects your mind to your body but without fear of scrutiny from others. A notebook is a safe space for you to explore what you truly think so that you can make choices rooted in your own wants and needs without external influence.

For that reason, you'll find lots of journal prompts throughout this book. Write down the answers that come up for you and spend some time journaling about the associated feelings. If at any time you feel upset by what comes up, take a break, get some fresh air, move your body, or talk to a friend and come back to the work in your own time. When I host writing workshops, I always tell my writers to give themselves permission to write truthfully, to let the words flow onto the page without judgement. I invite you to do the same.

Sometimes I'll draw your attention to a particular tip or action point, which can be found in boxes throughout the book. When you want to dive in and pull out practical tools to help you in the moment, these are a great starting point.

In line with my millennial nature, I've also included some listicle-style boxes because they're easy to digest and, to be honest, fun to write.

At the end of each section there is a reminder of the key takeaways which should spur you on to think about your next steps, even if that's just writing a list of things you want to consider or reflect on at a future date.

There is no race with this journey.

PART ONE
PAST

My story began before the digital age, but I'm sharing it because it illustrates the "before" version of myself, the girl who was passionately creative and a fearless performer, the girl who was unashamedly proud of her talents and often unfazed by societal pressures. But it will also give you a front row seat to witness how I veered off course, chose to do what was expected of me and landed myself in a career that felt critically off-balance. All this because I unknowingly became disconnected from the things that make me who I am, which had a deep-rooted impact on my mental health to the point where I had a mental breakdown. Things were falling apart around me and I barely noticed, because I wasn't watching for the signals, wasn't opening up to those around me and chose to hide from what was really going on.

The aim of this part of my story is to help you think deeply about what it is you want – and don't want – from life and how to move forward if you realize you're not where you're supposed to be. I'm going to gently challenge you to look internally and do some inquisitive thinking about where you've been, where you are and where you're going. Don't worry, this isn't a solo pursuit. Staying connected to others and being honest with them is key, as is recognizing the early signs of burnout so that you can get the support you deserve. If you ever get lost, try to remember what made that little version of you feel connected to the world. That person holds so many answers to the big questions about who you are becoming.

CHAPTER ONE

Before work became my downfall, before I figured out that connection was the answer, before celebrities became presidents, before isolation taught us all how to squish our lives into an online space, I grew up in a world without the internet.

Being raised in the late 1980s gave me a front-row seat to watch the world of social media unfold right before my very eyes in my young adult years. It almost feels like I've lived two lives: one before the internet existed and one as part of the digital age.

Like most children my interests were simple. I was curious and creative. I wanted to make things, whether that was dance routines to accompany my Spice Girls album, scripts written on an old typewriter, or gruesome drawings of haunted houses and witches.

Some of my fondest memories of my childhood are of sitting at a small, red plastic table and drawing pictures of my family while my brothers wrestled on the floor beside me. Whenever my mum (who is a naturally gifted artist herself) found me walking aimlessly around the house, feet dragging behind me, she would say, "What's wrong?" and I'd answer with a long monotonous drone, "I'm boooorreeddd." Her

5

10 signs you lived pre-internet

1. You can still recite your best friend's home phone number from when you were at school.

2. The sound of a dial-up connection gives you flashbacks to your mum interrupting your MSN flirting marathons.

3. You're willing to forgive members of the older generation who think that LOL means "lots of love".

4. There are large portions of your life that are only documented by a handful of photographs that were captured on a disposable camera.

5. Your first online learning experience was with a CD-ROM encyclopaedia that you checked out from the local library.

6. You've used a fully functioning public payphone multiple times in your life.

7. If required, you could knock up an acceptable last-minute birthday card using Clip Art and Microsoft Word.

8. Your backup email address is either Hotmail, Yahoo or AOL.

9. The first piece of tech you owned was a scientific calculator.

10. You still have a chequebook somewhere, just in case.

response was always something creative like, "Read a book," "Write a story" or, my personal favourite, "Take your pencil for a walk."

My love for creativity morphed into music too, spurred on by my dad's love of classic rock artists like Queen and Bruce Springsteen, which meant I could often be heard belting out a banger from the back seat of the car. At school I sang in shows and took part in the choir, getting a few solo performances under my belt before I left primary school. When the crowd applauded, I knew I'd done something important and any nerves that had rumbled behind the scenes were quickly forgotten.

All my female idols were pretty, gentle, quiet. So when the Spice Girls came along it was like they had crashed the tea party and made a glorious mess. They taught us that women could have a personality, a style that suits them and have what they really, really want. I took my lead from Geri Halliwell, the sassy, loud one who couldn't sing particularly well but gave it a good go nonetheless. One year for Halloween I dressed up as Ginger Spice and made all my mates rehearse a song for weeks so we could perform it in harmony when we went trick or treating. As I marched down the street wearing a Union Jack T-shirt and knock-off platform trainers to meet the rest of my bandmates, I felt the best I'd ever felt as a kid. Not because I was wearing quirky clothes or makeup for the first time, and certainly not because I was pretending to be someone else. It was because I was feeling unashamedly proud of who I was in that moment. I distinctly remember being ridiculously happy with the person I was that night, and I took on the brazen confidence that was displayed by my pop star idol without a second thought.

The Spice Girl energy that infiltrated my youth was the special sauce that pushed me to perform, even as a chubby ten-year-old. I had the confidence and optimism that comes from being told that girls can be whatever they want to be.

Dad was wearing a shirt and tie and carrying his leather briefcase as I pushed my cereal bowl to one side and pulled my chair in closer to the traditional typewriter set up on our kitchen table. A whiff of soap and pine followed him out of the door as he left on a Saturday morning to visit a construction site that needed a job looked at. Working in the building trade meant that the only unusual additions to his attire were a yellow hard hat and steel toe-capped boots; other than that, he was my first glimpse at the typical modern worker. Monday to Friday with a healthy dose of overtime.

I began using his typewriter just because I enjoyed the dramatically loud mechanical punching sound it made whenever I pressed a key. I-AM-TYPING. THIS-IS-FUN.

It made me feel like I was doing something meaningful, that I had ideas worthy of public consumption. I enjoyed the process of manually feeding in a new sheet of blank paper, staring at it longingly, and wondering what story I would write that day. Sometimes I wrote letters to my idols, like Geri Halliwell and Emma Bunton. Interestingly, I recently learned that this artistic version of correspondence – an attempt to redefine letter writing as a playful activity – is a technique recommended for adults who are looking to reconnect with their inner child. Some psychologists believe that the self we present to the world is false, one we create to fit in socially. Play is the tool used to connect with and gain awareness of the authentic self who lives underneath, the true emotional self. I suppose letter writing was a form of therapy for me as a teenager, even though I didn't realize it at the time.

Mum pottered around me, tidying up the dishes and talking about the weekend ahead. My younger brother Colin came stomping through in his muddy football boots only to be shimmied out of the back door with instructions to take them off and wipe himself down. From the other end of the house, the faint thump of terrible techno music filtered through from my older brother Stuart's room. Not quite a teenager but no longer a child, he was growing out of the playful games that I lived for.

Distractions were minimal with no email notifications, no funny cat compilations on YouTube, no Facebook friends, and definitely no smartphone to suck up all my time. I lost hours that day, writing a tale about some imaginary world, while Dad worked a normal job, and I still had the naïvety to dream that I wouldn't meet the same future. With a stack of blank paper and the future stretched out ahead of me, I could play at being whoever I wanted with no obstructions in the way. I was the author of my own story. Who could stop me?

Writing wasn't the only thing that made me feel invincible. I entered my art into competitions, content in the knowledge that I had just as much right as anyone else to be considered for the prize. When I won a local drawing competition, I stood proudly for the photographers and got butterflies when I saw it printed in the newspaper. The book token I received as a prize went toward Roald Dahl stories that inspired me to keep writing, which I continued to do all through primary school. I sang solo in front of audiences without the worry of being laughed at. People told me I was talented and I believed them.

As an adult, all those things would now terrify me. But there's value in looking back at those chances we took when we were young and full of wonder. We didn't let the fear of failure stop us from trying, we did things because we enjoyed them, regardless of the outcome. We were connected to our true wants and desires, and the sad reality is that those seem to become buried deeper and deeper the older we get.

CONNECTING WITH YOUR CHILDHOOD PASSIONS

What could you do if failure or humiliation didn't bother you? Would you follow your instincts and try new things? Be honest about what you're truly fanatical about?

Your childhood passion for baking cupcakes doesn't necessarily mean that you're destined to be a patisserie chef, but it could direct you to the things that motivate you to do certain things. Perhaps you like the fun of seeking out the best recipe (researching, problem solving), or the act of making a beautiful cupcake (creativity, attention to detail), or maybe it's seeing the smile on your friend's face when they took their first bite (presenting, customer relations). The soft skills that came naturally to you as a child are transferable into the working world, and if you're not using them in your current job, is that something you'd like to change? And by the way, I'm not saying that the thing you loved as a child is automatically connected to the thing you should be doing as a job as an adult. Not everyone who did cartwheels at school is destined to do gymnastics at the Olympics. My love for performing didn't lead me into a career as a pop star. But an awareness of the things that brought you joy as a child is always helpful, enlightening, perhaps thought-provoking ... and can open you up to allowing yourself to play with new pathways and a deeper sense of happiness when you trace your current life backwards, retracing your steps to see where it all began.

During the last few months of primary school, we were all being prepped for "big school" and part of that was talking about the future. The final few days were set aside for a celebration, but we'd also be doing an assembly to show all the adoring parents what we were looking forward to after graduation.

Gathered, cross-legged on the scratchy carpet, the teacher had a special project for us. We were tasked with rewriting the entire lyrics of "When I'm Sixty-Four" – he was an avid Beatles fan – customizing every line to correspond with a pupil in our class, and making an effort to talk about which profession we wanted to go into as an adult. Being asked to write a song from the perspective of my future 64-year-old self should have terrified me at a mere 12 years old, but that felt like a long way off. My future was bright and I was ready to commit that sentiment to music.

CHAPTER ONE

One by one, the teacher made his way around the circle of eager faces.

"What do you want to be when you grow up?"

David said he wanted to be a roofer and the teacher nodded in approval.

Bonnie said that she wanted to be a nurse and the teacher raised a palm to his heart in admiration.

Gareth stuttered for a moment and then said quietly that he would be a farmer, just like his dad. The teacher accepted this without question, as though the path had already been paved and he was merely herding the boy in the right direction.

Rolling my eyes, I waited my turn. Where were all the astronauts? The explorers? The chocolate tasters? They had all chosen such boring jobs.

As time edged closer, I tried to think about what I would say. What were my interests? Where did my skills lie? What was I good at, and did that even matter? What made me tick? Could I make a difference in the world?

I know now that not everyone has the privilege of doing a job they are proud of. For the majority, work is a necessity, a form of survival. It does nothing to reflect the attributes of a person, their kindness, loyalty, ability to tell a good joke or tuck you in at night. Asking children what they want to be when they grow up plants the idea that your job is the sole thing that defines you. Adults are saying: "Tell us what you want to be so that we can tell you you're good."

So, is it any wonder that we grow up hooked on the need to prove our worth by chasing promotions and titles and new jobs that we don't actually want? None of these thoughts were yet conscious in my childhood mind, but when the figurative microphone landed in front of my face, I got stage fright. Surrounded by my peers who planned to take career paths that made them unquestionably helpful to society, I tried to pinpoint what I'd been doing with my time … which was mostly writing silly wee stories, doodling and performing on stage. I was torn and didn't know what to do, and I was embarrassed to admit that the jobs I wanted to do were fun and frivolous. The teacher would probably think I was stupid or selfish.

Channelling my inner girl power, I took a deep breath and laid out my two dream careers for my teacher. I asked what he thought was best. (Asking a middle-aged man what I should do with my life probably wasn't what the Spice Girls would have wanted, but I was struggling). Which path should I take?

"I either want to be an author or a pop star," I said with trepidation.

He nodded sympathetically and I braced myself for bad news.

"Well," he clasped his hands together, "I don't see why you need to pick just one thing. You can do both."

On the last day, I stood up there with no idea of who I wanted to be, really, but I sang along to the terrible Beatles cover we'd butchered and thought about all the possibilities ahead of me. On the way out I waved goodbye to my teacher, not fully appreciating how much I needed someone to tell me that it was OK to have options. That there was more than one way to build a career.

I could quite often be found every evening sprawled out on my Spice Girls bedsheets writing in my diary, which thankfully came complete with the world's tiniest padlock.

Along with writing in my diary, I went through a lengthy period of my teenage years where I was always writing letters. My mum encouraged the idea, along with taking my pen for a walk, knowing that it would keep me quiet for a few minutes while I jotted down my exciting life over a few lavender-scented pages. I was always very fond of writing letters and as a result, I acquired pen pals throughout the years who I would stay in contact with by post.

I pulled out all the stops you might imagine a teenager with my disposition for drama would. I bought new paper, envelopes, pens and stickers to make every letter stand out. I spent hours pouring my heart out in each carefully constructed note. I decorated every envelope with glitter pens and drawings, and sprayed them with my favourite Tommy Girl perfume to truly personalize each piece of correspondence.

Any writer will tell you that they regularly set out to write about a particular subject, with a specific angle, only to find themselves wandering into new territory which often results in an element of self-discovery. It's often not until you read back what you've written that you realize you arrived at the page to say something to yourself that you didn't even know was rattling around inside of you. Toward the end of high school, I moved away from letter writing as cellphones became commonplace and PCs were available in almost every home. Instead of writing letters to my friends, I was communicating mostly through text messages on my top-of-the-range Nokia 5110, which could only store a total of ten messages but was somehow still too big to fit in my pocket. When I inevitably ran out of credit (of course I did, I'm a writer – every text message was limited to 459 characters and I had a lot to say), everything would end abruptly with nocreditleftsoz. Then I would use the next best thing: MSN Messenger.

Most families like us only had one shared computer, which was set up in a communal area – for us it was the dining room – and we all had to take turns in getting to use it.

8 ways to pursue your childhood passions as an adult

1. *Go to a university open day to find out about courses in your area of interest.*
2. *Start your own local meet-up group for people who have similar interests.*
3. *Browse the library for books on subjects you want to learn more about.*
4. *Check your local newspaper for events.*
5. *Find like-minded people in Facebook groups.*
6. *Ask your employer if they offer any funding for you to go on training courses or attend seminars in your chosen field.*
7. *Write a list of all the activities you'd like to try and schedule them into your calendar throughout the year.*
8. *Share this list with friends and ask if anyone would like to join you.*

Everyone around that time was seriously addicted to MSN, and I particularly enjoyed it because I could use it to talk to other people without feeling nervous. By this time, I'd been at high school for a few years and my youthful tenacity had started to fade away. I suppose I was slightly more anxious than the average 15-year-old girl and wanted to portray the coolest vibe possible around potential love interests. Talking to people with a screen between us was a dream come true, because I've always been more comfortable expressing myself in writing than any other form. I could write out funny jokes, reference obscure bands and quote comments straight out of the latest issue of NME pretending that they were my own interesting opinions. The cloak of coolness was easier to brandish from behind a screen.

Before long, I was spending all my spare time and money on music. I took part in any music group that would have me, which meant singing show tunes as part of school productions, Christmas carols with the choir and forming my own rock band with some boys in my year. Every week I took piano lessons but never managed to connect with the instrument to get particularly good at playing it. On the other hand, I just loved singing because it came naturally to me, but I also felt particularly connected to music as a form of expression as a young adult. I would spend hours in my bedroom reading lyrics by bands like Coldplay and Keane (granted, I wasn't the trendiest) and feeling part of something bigger, especially when I felt like someone else in the world was writing a song about exactly how I felt at that same time. I got into older bands like Guns N' Roses and tried to like Bob Dylan too, but settled on easier listening like Bruce

Springsteen and Neil Young, who are still two of my all-time favourite artists.

Years later, I still find myself gravitating toward the soundtrack of my youth because it's so comforting. In 2020, during lockdown, I found myself circling back to music as a main priority. I would spend hours in the bath, periodically topping up the hot water, carefully listening to albums from start to finish. Transported back to the days when my main worries were what top I was going to wear to the school disco and would I have enough time to finish my homework in registration class. Hearing the music that accompanied my teenage years reminded me of the unspoken certainty I had within me. I may not have felt outwardly confident, but internally I was self-assured in one thing. Creativity was my calling, I was sure of that.

CHAPTER TWO

There was no discussion about what my future would entail. The plan wasn't designed by me, it already existed. Go to school, study hard, get the best results you can, enjoy extracurricular activities, pick your career path, apply for university, go to university, graduate and you'll be rewarded with a job in your chosen industry.

The alternative? I don't remember ever having that conversation.

Age 15 and the time for self-discovery was over as I sat opposite the teacher tasked with guiding me through the preparation process for higher education. My tie hung loosely around my neck, a fat knot that was supposed to show that I didn't really care about school, that I was mature enough to be out in the real world. Friendly eyes from the teacher and I knew what was coming. The question about what I want to be when I grow up. Shuffling of documents, tapping on keys and then he opened his mouth to say, "So what career options are you considering?"

His delivery threw me off. There was no "when you grow up" and no patronizing tone. He waited for my response, like he believed I was the person with all the answers. Mumbling something about music, writing and creativity, my bravado was fading. What saved me in the end was the promise of admin. There were quizzes to be taken, boxes to be checked, options to be weighed up, subjects to choose, skills to develop, personal statements to be drafted, applications to be made and open days to attend. Lost under a mountain of paperwork and possibilities, I took it one step at a time and ended up somewhere that felt inevitable and easy which, at the time, seemed like the best place to be.

Writing was comfortable, came naturally to me and felt like a sensible option that would lead me to a newspaper or maybe into teaching. It made sense, I guess and the guidance teacher approved. On the other hand, music was fun and had a fiery urgency that burned in me every day. I was playing in bands, singing live, writing music and listening to anything I could get my hands on but, of course, the job prospects were … OK I'll be honest, I didn't fully look into the job prospects before I sent in my application. But exploring the creativity in music felt so exciting that when I was offered a place to study Commercial Music without the need to achieve any other grades, there was no doubt in my mind that my answer was yes.

The three years that followed were a blur of cheap cider, library visits, late afternoon lectures and live music. The collaborative tasks set on the course were challenging, but they pushed me creatively in the way that I'd dreamed of when I sat in that musty careers office trying to conjure up a vision for my life.

The first year saw us divided up into groups where we had to form a band, write a collection of songs and perform them live at the end of term. I was no longer the best singer in the vicinity and I felt self-conscious being surrounded by literally hundreds of wildly talented musicians. I was beginning to get chronically nervous before stepping on stage, but it was somehow more achievable as part of a group and the fact that it was part of my course material. Push through, grin and get the grade. Stick to the plan.

I'd like to say that I honed my skills as a lead vocalist throughout my university years, or that I mastered the art of sound recording while penning some hit singles along the way. The truth is that I realized quite early on in my degree that although I enjoyed the course content, fitted in with my peers, and could belt out a good tune, something didn't feel quite right.

During the practical elements of the course, I watched as one guy picked up a trumpet for the first time in his life and figured out how to play it in less than ten minutes. I sat on the bench outside my halls of residence as a group of students lugged equipment into a rehearsal room and emerged an hour later with a handful of songs ready to perform that evening. One woman in the year above set herself up as a manager and got a band a record deal. Instead of feeling invigorated by everyone else's encyclopaedic knowledge and musical intuition, I felt left out. I knew that eventually I would leave the party and no one would miss me. The intense hopefulness I'd had as a kid was slowly diluting, and I was beginning to wonder if the music industry was really the place I was built for, and if not, where else could I go?

While many of my fellow students were specializing in business management or events organization, I only found one class that I was particularly interested in and it was only for one semester – Music Journalism. The writing flowed easily and although I didn't always have a clue what or who I was writing about, I could at least craft something of interest using the one thing I was a natural at – the written language. Words were my guitar, my drums, my bass. Words were the thing I could pick up and play with relative ease and it provided some relief among the tide of sparkly musicians I compared myself with every day.

I made a special request to change some of my music modules to journalism classes, which were part of another course. My lecturer could see that I was putting in effort with my writing so he signed off my request and I did another two writing classes, throwing myself in with bags of enthusiasm by teaming up with a fellow writer to produce a few issues of our own music zine. When the journalism lecturer recommended that I spearhead a one-off edition of the university newspaper, I jumped at the chance. I still have my copy of *Papercuts* saved in a folder under my bed; one of the early signs that I cared more about writing than anything else.

These little morsels gave me a taste for writing, but the course as a whole didn't provide any further sustenance, so in my third year I took a part-time job in a local café. Soon enough, I was becoming more and more excited about heading there on a Saturday to serve coffees and cakes than I was about completing my degree. I had a fair bit of responsibility in the café too; I was a key-holder and was running my own shifts whenever the manager wasn't there. I knew that when I showed up to work, there was a specific job to do and if I simply followed my training and worked hard, I would be rewarded. Better shifts on the rota, a pay rise, perhaps another promotion down the line. The validation of having a real job massaged my ego and suddenly, spending hours in the university library typing up articles to cut and paste into my handmade music zines felt immature. I'd rather be doing an extra shift in the café, getting paid in cold hard cash for my work.

It was the morning after one such shift and I was slumped in a chair at the front of the classroom. Long, slow blinks offered temporary respite as the course leader leaned on the desk at the front, greeting other students by name and referring to a gig that had taken place in the union the night before. I had no idea what they were talking about.

"OK, settle down folks," he closed the door and began talking in a serious tone, "I'm here to talk to you about fourth year."

Stifling a groan, I rolled my eyes and closed the notebook I'd just opened up in preparation for learning. Thinking about next year was too much, couldn't we just deal with that after summer? We had loads of time.

"Now, I know it seems like a long way off but you'll need to start thinking about your dissertation topic and talk over those ideas with your assigned supervisor as soon as possible. You'll want to figure out your research methods, reading list ..."

His voice faded into nothing as I pictured another year of this, another year of working toward something meaningless, another year of trying to achieve a grade that I didn't care about. But leaving at the end of the third year meant giving up. My degree would technically still count, but it would be missing a few important

CHAPTER TWO

letters at the end that were a requirement for so many job applications.

"And another thing," he took a step closer to my desk, "your final year does not allow space for a part-time job. You need to think long and hard about whether you can dedicate the time and energy required to achieve an honours degree."

I swapped a side glance with a girl next to me. Giving up my job, losing money, and continuing down this path just felt wrong on so many levels. I had to get out.

REFLECTIVE JOURNALING PROMPTS

Before you make a big decision, such as picking a university, accepting a job offer, moving to a new city, ending a relationship, committing to an existing one, journal on these questions to connect to what you really want:

1. *Is this really what you want, or are you doing it because you think you "should"?*
2. *Will this decision have a positive/negative impact on the people you get to connect with?*
3. *What are the short-term/long-term financial implications of this decision?*
4. *How do your natural personality traits play into this decision?*
5. *How will the outcome of this decision impact your energy levels?*
6. *How will this impact your current hobbies?*
7. *What is motivating you to go ahead with this decision?*
8. *What is pulling you away from this decision?*
9. *If this opportunity was off the table, what would you do instead?*

CHAPTER THREE

Photographs at the graduation ceremony were taken in quick succession, like a production line of baby adults who didn't know whether to smile or scream at the camera. The room was filled with hundreds of faces that I didn't recognize because I was graduating a year before everyone else in my class. I had found two other women from my course who were, like me, cutting their losses and making a run for it, and we had laughed and congratulated each other after walking on stage to collect our certificates. Most people waved exuberantly at family members who whooped from the audience below, but I stared at my feet the whole time, only looking up to shake the hand of some middle-aged white man who told me I had done well.

Cameras flashed and the crowd around me rumbled with conversation, Dad tapped me on the shoulder and nodded toward the front of the room where the photographer beckoned me over. It was my turn. He handed me a paper scroll and I clutched it between sweaty palms and tried to look proud of myself. Out of the corner of my eye I could see my parents watching, beaming. When I gave back the scroll, I saw it was just a scrap piece of paper with some random booking confirmation on one side. Curled into the shape of something meaningful.

Outside, the car park swarmed with other graduates in sweeping black gowns, sipping champagne and hugging family members. I waved goodbye to the women on my course and took off the robe as soon as I got into the car. We spent the evening celebrating with my boyfriend Joe (we'd been dating since we met in freshers' week), drinking cocktails, eating at a fancy seafood restaurant and talking about university life as though it was already a forgotten dream. Success wasn't in the air for me that day; it was more a sense of relief that one part of my life was over and the next part had permission to begin.

All the extra shifts I'd done in the café paid off when, directly after graduation, I was offered an Assistant Manager role. Seattle café culture had made its way over to the UK, but Starbucks had yet to have a store on every corner, so the chain I worked for was growing quickly due to lack of competition. It had a trendy vibe with live music nights twice a week, indie records at the till, huge squishy leather sofas and mugs that required two hands to carry without spilling.

The work was boring (serving customers, cleaning, making coffees, counting money) but the days passed quickly. When I locked the door at 11pm, my work was done. When I returned to my flat-share with another student I would find her passed out on the sofa surrounded by textbooks and flashcards, revising endlessly for exams that I would never need to worry about again. Crawling into bed smelling of stale coffee had never felt so good.

Six months later, I was offered a promotion. To relocate to Glasgow to manage my own store, one of their busiest flagship cafés. Success was on the horizon and although it was a far cry from those creative jobs I had dreamed about in primary school, it felt real, proper. Something that would prove my abilities to the world. The plan was coming together, albeit in a slightly different way than originally intended, but who cared? If I could have the status and salary of an adult, then everything would be fine. I would be safe.

The official job offer came to my work email and I opened it during a quiet afternoon lull. As I skim-read through the words, *store manager, relocation, salary increase*, I had to stand up and shake off the energy fizzing through my bones. Excitement. Panic.

I paced around the kitchen of the café. Distracted myself by clearing tables, sweeping up crumbs, straightening chairs, and rearranging muffins and pastries until I could no longer ignore the question in my mind. Why did my employers think I would be capable of this job in the first place? I definitely couldn't do this job.

All my friends were still studying so there was no one in my immediate circle that I could turn to for advice. The business books I had read were written by male CEOs who had no patience for people who felt like they weren't worthy of promotion, so I followed their lead and chose hard work over admitting any signs of weakness. I summoned all the energy I could muster, marched back into the office and accepted the job offer before I had a chance to change my mind.

Weeks later, I was standing in my own store – nestled in Glasgow's West End – which I quickly learned was swarming with customers from open until close, leaving little time for anything other than a quick bite to eat and one toilet break per shift. To counteract the lack of self-belief that still grumbled in my gut, I did endless unpaid overtime, diligently filled out pointless paperwork, dusted fake plants, jabbed temperature probes into stale muffins, and scrubbed baby sick off the floor with a smile.

Within a year, the recession began to control everything. Bosses told me in no uncertain terms that my priority was to minimize spending, which meant I had to cut everyone's hours and fill in any gaps on the rota by working the hours myself. As a salaried employee, this meant working more hours but getting no paid overtime, so that 12-hour shifts and six-day weeks became the norm. Restaurants and shops on

6 QUESTIONS TO ASK YOURSELF WHEN YOU'RE OFFERED A PROMOTION

This exercise is designed to help you inquire into your own thought process and feelings toward the situation. If you don't want the promotion but feel you "need" it because of financial reasons, that's OK. Just be aware of these feelings and make your decision with them in mind.

1. *Do I really want this job or am I just flattered to be asked?*
2. *Will this job lead me to a place I actually want to go?*
3. *What are the main benefits of the promotion?*
4. *What are the downsides?*
5. *Is the extra responsibility worth the pay rise?*
6. *Am I mentally prepared for the role?*

our street began to close. Customers were few and far between and as unemployment rose, they started spending less. Profits were lean.

The area manager popped into the store unannounced regularly, and I constantly felt on edge waiting for her to walk in and tell me that my standards weren't up to scratch. Even though I worked as much as I could, I never seemed to meet her requirements, so I always felt sick with fear, a dull fluttering in my gut as a reminder that I was never, ever going to be good enough.

It was a chilly spring afternoon when I sat down with whatever sandwich I had cobbled together with leftovers, and as I took the first bite I saw the area manager stride in, subtly surveying the surroundings. She knew all the vulnerable places in every unit: the corners that were most likely to need scrubbing, the gaps behind the fridge that trapped food fragments, the one sugar bowl that wasn't immaculate and filled with equal amounts of sugar and sweetener sachets. All my errors exposed.

Swallowing a bite of my sandwich in one dry gulp, I simultaneously scanned the shop for flaws she could pick up on. They were imperceptible to everyone else, but I knew for certain that they were peppered everywhere. A dusty corner in the bathrooms that no one ever wiped, an almost empty soap dispenser in the kitchen that I had planned to refill an hour ago, and the empty fridge that had yet to be restocked after lunch. With less staff on the rota, this was always the way. I waved hello to her and let her wander around, doing her usual inspection, as I resisted the urge to run over and fall on my knees and plead forgiveness. Quietly and quickly I finished lunch then slipped into the kitchen, tidied up and refilled the soap, and instructed my colleague to take care of the fridge display. When I turned around the area manager was standing in front of me, so close her perfume clung to my apron. It smelled musky, expensive. She adjusted her oversized leather bag on her shoulder and frowned, her eyes betraying her in a way that made me feel sweaty and unattractive. I wasn't a proper career woman like her, but maybe if I impressed her enough, I could get close.

"No time to chat," she said with false sympathy, "heading down the coast for the weekend." She put on a pair of Gucci sunglasses and left. Less than an hour later I received an email from her which listed all the ways in which I'd failed to keep the store up to her standards. She had every right to pull me up on genuine mistakes, but it seemed to me that she was seeking a level of perfection that was unattainable. Yet I bent over backwards to try and prove I could reach it. My success at work depended on it.

Instead of asking for support or admitting that I wasn't coping, I dug my heels in and tried to raise my game. I was always on the prowl, waiting for staff members to make a mistake and, as a result, small conflicts were blown out of proportion. This was anxiety at its finest, heightening all my senses, making me catastrophize tiny errors, such as an overflowing bin or a spelling mistake on the specials board. On a rare day off, I often planned my day around a visit to my store so that I could check that the staff weren't skiving. When I made my presence known, no one jumped, no one apologized for the mess. No one cared.

RED FLAGS THAT SIGNAL A TOXIC WORK CULTURE

Being aware of triggers can help you tap into why you might be feeling unfulfilled at work. Instead of blaming yourself, look around and observe if certain situations or people are impeding your ability to enjoy work. Connecting with how you feel at work can help you make decisions about how to support yourself in all areas of your life.

- *Poor communication*
- *Feedback and complaints are never taken seriously*
- *Lack of connection within your team*
- *Disinterested employees*
- *Poor staff retention*
- *Constant monitoring and lack of trust in employees*

I later learned this was hypervigilance, an elevated state of arousal in which you constantly assess your surroundings for potential threats. It can cause sleep problems and angry outbursts and is a symptom of post-traumatic stress disorder (PTSD). In late 2021, the NHS anticipated approximately 230,000 new cases of PTSD in the UK as a result of COVID-19.

On one occasion when I popped in to do a surprise check-up, I ended up having a blazing argument with a lazy staff member in front of customers, ironically rendering me the worst employee on my entire team.

I stormed home and cried for an hour and couldn't bear the shame of how I'd behaved, so, at 11am in the morning, I opened a bottle of beer because I needed to forget about how I'd acted, and I wanted to shake off this feeling that had been lingering for months.

I just didn't feel myself.

I was out of control, angry.

I didn't like who I was becoming.

The big explosion had come just a few days after I'd been put through a formal disciplinary procedure in response to a visit from my area manager who reported an unclean toilet seat. It was my day off, I wasn't on shift when the "incident" occurred, but I was the boss, so the blame lay with me. I took my formal warning on the chin, gave a genuine apology and tried to do better.

But now I was sobbing and drinking daytime beer all alone and I had to admit that maybe it was time to cut my losses. It was time to look for a new job.

I spent all day updating my CV and applying for other management jobs. If there was a café, retail outlet or office looking for someone with management experience, then I applied. Weeks passed and I received nothing but rejections, so I widened my search to include lower-paying jobs and supervisor roles. Still, no takers. In the end, I put my name forward for anything full-time and finally, I had a job interview for a catering outlet in a Glasgow tourist attraction where I could earn just above minimum wage.

In the interview, I explained that no, this wasn't a stopgap, that yes, I'd been looking for management roles but couldn't find anything to match my experience. With unemployment at an unprecedented high, it was true: there were simply too many over-qualified workers and not enough jobs to go around. My case stated, we shook hands and I left feeling disappointed that I'd used a paid holiday day for this. Being grilled about my work history knowing that it would likely result in another "thanks, but no thanks".

The sun glistened on the River Clyde as I walked away from the opportunity, back to my life where monotony beckoned. Was I crazy for even considering leaving a well-paid job when the economy was this unstable? Did my happiness at work really matter as much as putting money in my bank account? I'd be losing status with a minimum wage job, there would be no glory, no buzz in announcing this new role to friends and family.

It was a Friday afternoon when I got the call and I heard those four words that sounded like hope: "When can you start?"

When I handed in my notice at the coffee shop, the area manager said she would be sad to see me go.

I heard her say the words, but her eyes didn't seem to match the sentiment. We had a brief chat where I finally admitted the truth to her: "I'm not management material," I said, without an ounce of regret.

Her brow furrowed in genuine bemusement: "But you're so good at it, Fiona."

But it didn't really matter what she said, what kind of compliments she threw at my feet. My mind was already made up.

BURNOUT

The symptoms of burnout often creep in so slowly over time that you may not even notice they're happening. Reconnect with yourself right now while reading this list of physical and emotional red flags associated with burnout:

- *Easily agitated*
- *Feeling overwhelmed*
- *Perceived inability to work efficiently*
- *Constantly tired*
- *Insomnia*
- *Unexplained aches and pains*
- *Feelings of hopelessness, loneliness, detachment*
- *Self-medicating with food, drugs or alcohol*

Months passed as I settled into my new role as a catering assistant. I made coffees, stocked fridges, and served sandwiches and fried chips with a cheerfulness that I'd forgotten was possible at work. The simplicity of the tasks was a breath of fresh air and the routine actions, falling into a groove, reminded me of tapping on that old typewriter. I was creating a world that I wanted to live in.

On one rainy national holiday, the café was overrun with hungry families looking for clean tables and hot food. Filthy highchairs blocked exits and bins overflowed with paper cups and sticky wrappers. From the edges, I watched the supervisor dash around dealing with customer complaints while keeping one eye on the other staff members who were growing wearier by the minute. I moved quickly and did my best to serve everyone with a smile and inside I was surprisingly calm, something that I had never experienced on a busy shift in my old job. Hours later, when I was putting on my jacket to leave, the head of the department walked past and acknowledged me with a smile.

"Well done today," he punched my shoulder playfully, "you're definitely management material!" I tried to stifle my pride as he walked away, inwardly beaming at the warmth of recognition. Always flattered by a person in power who tells me I'm worth something.

Meanwhile, I was sneaking into the staff room on my lunch breaks to pilfer instant coffee and tea bags to take home because my income was dangerously low. I'd underestimated how much travel costs would eat into my monthly wage packet and was walking an hour each way to save on buying a subway ticket. When the soles in my shoes began to wear out, I started to worry.

A few months later I was offered a promotion.

The whiff of success was in the air once again, but I knew deep down that I didn't really want to be in charge, I didn't want the extra responsibility. Maybe the stress, the bouts of anger that came before were just a one-off. I genuinely believed that this time would be different, and the extra money would mean I could afford to live more comfortably. The lure of appearing to have my life in order was too tempting to refuse.

So, I accepted the promotion, relaxed into the role and found that I was capable of balancing life and work without too much trouble. The company had pre-existing systems and procedures that made my job relatively straightforward. Until one day, my boss and I were chatting over coffee about an upcoming delivery. "I've got to check this in, then I've got a training session, a performance meeting, and that's before I even get started on the rota."

Keen to please and looking for something to do, I volunteered to do the staff rota for him.

"I used to do it in my old job," I shrugged.

"That would be such a big help," he admitted, but still dubious about whether I could perform the task at hand. "Give it a go, then I'll double-check it for you."

From that moment on, the rota was my responsibility. Every week I was given an afternoon in the office to input everything into the computer and communicate the rota to the team. As the weeks progressed I picked up other managerial tasks that, in my eyes, were no hassle to add to my day. Delivering staff training, phoning suppliers, running meetings. It all felt so easy.

Joe and I were going strong and enjoying living together in our first flat, in the heart of Glasgow's bustling west end. We had our pick of cool bars, restaurants and music venues, not to mention art galleries and beautiful parks to explore when the weather allowed.

But my career still wasn't taking off in the direction I had hoped.

Supervising wasn't particularly challenging, but wasn't all that drama exactly what I'd been so keen to escape from in my previous job? Wasn't the stress-free life the one I'd been fantasizing about? I had to admit that all this plain sailing was starting to feel unsatisfying.

In the evenings, I searched for creative jobs and dreamed about going back to university, studying journalism or creative writing. I found a bursary scheme for night classes and did some writing sessions at a local university, which I enjoyed, but taking that next step to make it into a career felt like pie in the sky. I had tried all that. My degree in music proved to me that I wasn't passionate enough to have an artistic job, I was destined to be in middle management and hate my job the majority of the time. Everyone hated their job, right? There was no evidence to suggest that I was smart or talented enough to break that mould.

When the opportunity for *yet another, slightly more scary* promotion came up, I put my name forward. With a big career box waiting to be ticked, this could be my chance to boost my confidence and prove my worth. Excitement and fulfilment beckoned.

On the day of the interview, I asked to be excused five minutes before my meeting so that I could change out of my uniform into a pencil skirt and blouse. During the interview, my boss posed questions about team-building and customer retention. I asked for a glass of water to buy me some time and when he reached over for the bottle I noticed my reflection in the glass door. My cheeks and chest were scarlet red, and I caught a whiff of sweat that was collecting in my armpits. The rest of the interview felt clunky when I was unable to formulate responses that conveyed my experience, and my general appearance made me too self-conscious to fully relax. Blustering through the conversation, I couldn't wait to escape and get back to my existing role.

By the time I got back to the bathroom to change, I was almost in tears, embarrassed that I had even thought I was capable of rising up the ranks again and annoyed for putting myself through the process. Panic was rising in my chest. Was it the fear of losing out or the fear of getting what I wanted?

Less than 24 hours later I was invited back into the same interview room and formally offered the job. It felt rude not to accept.

I had an office, with cheery yellow paintwork and a bathroom right across the hall. If only I had stopped to take it all in, to take a closer look at what I was running headfirst into, I might have seen the pattern, the events beginning to repeat themselves. But I didn't stop, I didn't open my eyes, I ran full steam ahead.

CHAPTER FOUR

It was the end of a life that fast-tracked the breakdown of my own.

When my dad rang – he never normally rang – I knew it was bad news but I didn't expect it to be the death of my gran. She lived a long life, so it shouldn't have been a surprise, but still, you never really prepare yourself for these moments, do you?

The day after I heard the news, I was scheduled to carry out job interviews for my department so I got up as usual, put on my makeup, wore a nice dress, styled my hair and acted professional. After the last candidate left the room, I gathered up my papers and calmly walked to the bathroom where no one could find me. I locked myself in my favourite stall and felt the urge to vomit, but nothing came up. I put the seat down and sat alone in the space and cried quietly for a few minutes. All I knew was that for once, no one was looking for me or asking me to come back to work. It felt like, somehow, they all knew that I was otherwise engaged and needed to be left alone.

When the tears eventually stopped, I exited the stall and looked at myself in the mirror and saw that my eyeliner flick was no longer in place but had, instead, slid down my cheek to meet my chin. Black smeared into the dry skin around my nose and I picked at it, trying to hide my messy reflection from myself. I wondered who the tears were really for, and if they had been waiting to surface long before today. Wiping away the blackened tears, I went back to work. A week later I took one day off to attend my gran's funeral and then got straight back into my routine as soon as possible.

During a conversation with Joe, he gently asked, "Don't you want to take a bit more time off?"

"I'm fine," was the answer because I was an expert at saying yes.

Yes, I want the distraction.

Yes, I want the praise.

Yes, I want anything other than the shame of resting.

Taking a sick day wasn't an option because that meant relinquishing the honour of being busy, stressed and pleasing everyone around me by carrying the workload.

Managing the two main catering outlets of the business – which often fed over 2,000 people per day – was depleting my resources. The trendy café I'd worked in before was forgiven for being a little "rough around the edges" by the majority of the clientele who just wanted a big coffee and a stable Wi-Fi connection, but this job required precision, confident leadership and the relentless pursuit of perfection. Parents were paying their hard-earned cash for a family day out. This could make or break their weekend, their summer holiday, so there was a lot of pressure to give them a five-star experience. I wanted so badly for my department to deliver the goods, but for every hundred positive reviews we received, there was always one negative one that stuck in my mind.

No highchairs available.

Spillage on the floor.

Poor sandwich selection.

Every day, I made a note of ways I needed to improve. Things that had to change in order for me to be better at my job, to make me a better person.

At home, things were moving in a more positive direction. Joe and I moved into my gran's old house so we now lived in a two-bedroom, semi-detached house with a garden. On the day we moved in I stood in the kitchen and looked out to the overgrown grass, the long-forgotten vegetable patch, the weeds sprouting up in between the paving. There was so much potential for growth. We didn't own it, but there was scope for that in the future which felt like the right thing to do, to have a plan, a goal in mind. My life was starting to look just as it was supposed to. Proper job, proper house, happy relationship.

Not long after we moved into our new home, the gift shop and cinema snack bar manager at my workplace retired. As he collected his things and handed in his keys and ID badge, I struggled to congratulate him on his newfound freedom and, instead, I jokingly begged him to stay. When he laughed and said no, I tried to hide my tears.

A week later, I took over his remit without question.

Having never managed a retail business before there was a lot of learning to do, but I could see my career, my life, progressing in an upwards direction and I was hooked on seeing what it looked like at the top.

Just as I was easing myself into my extra duties my boss suddenly left the business and I took over his role too, which included being the buyer for the entire company. So, the 26-year-old graduate, who had stumbled into a career in catering and had left her previous job because she was not "management material", now found herself managing three departments and three budgets, in charge of four supervisors, four rotas and 30 staff members, and had the job of purchasing hundreds of thousands of pounds worth of stock for the businesses that she had no clue how to run. There were lots of suppliers to speak to, often elderly men who had been dealing with my predecessors for close to a decade. I tried to haggle them down on pricing and return faulty items with varying success. Being a 20-something blonde woman was not working in my favour. People looked down on me because of my age, gender and perceived lack of experience. My calendar overflowed with appointments, leaving no scope for helping in the café on a busy day, so I was sneered at by the staff members too.

That sick, fluttering in my gut was back. And it was getting worse.

My friends had all graduated from university by this point and we were all in that honeymoon period of full-time employment where you've got endless energy to work 50 hours a week and party all weekend. Most of the time, I was too tired to go out dancing, so I opted for a bottle of wine in front of the TV.

The anxious, always-on feeling of work was starting to make sleeping a bit of a problem. Have you ever been so tired that you can't sleep? Yeah, that. Instead of investigating the root of the problem, I stuck a boozy Band-Aid on it and decided that some chemically induced shut-eye was better than none at all. Of course, I know now that this was never a restful sleep and often left me feeling more exhausted and rundown the next day, which perpetuated the cycle and made me reach for the Merlot yet again. My hair was limp and dry. For the first time in my life, I was losing weight without trying. Loud noises made me jump. Any minor inconvenience made me illogically angry.

I spent the next ten months in a cycle of self-destruction, drinking all weekend before turning up to work every Monday morning, without fail, ready to act like I had my shit together. Every day, my to-do list grew longer, more unwieldy, and my responsibilities for each job role I'd been lumbered with became more intense and I could see the cracks starting to appear whenever I looked in the mirror.

One Sunday morning in April, I stood barefoot in the back garden with my toes wriggling in the grass. On the right, the solid foundations where my grandpa's greenhouse used to stand, bursting with heat and zingy tomatoes fresh off the vine. On the left, a vast raised bed of upturned soil where he used to grow potatoes, sweet peas, carrots and salad leaves. Maybe one day I would have the time to plant my own seeds in there and nurture something to fruition. There were so many possibilities, but also, so much work to be done.

At 6am the next day I was awake and ready to take the two buses required to get to the office just before 9am. Leaning my head against the window, I tried to picture wildflowers growing in our garden but every time I drifted off, all I could picture was thorny weeds, twisting and curling around my hands, pinning me down and dragging me into the earth.

Today was about filing a stash of reports that had been on my to-do list for weeks, but time was running out and I needed to make them a priority. When I arrived in the office, there were already figurative fires burning. A voicemail from a sick staff member who wasn't coming into work, an enormous delivery in the basement and a broken goods lift that rendered it unreachable. At midday, I realized I was still wearing my coat. A small part of me knew that this was a sign, proof that I was moving too fast. But another part, the bigger part, puffed up her chest in pride. *Hard work means success,* I thought to myself as I shook off my coat, downed my third coffee of the day and rushed to a meeting with the head of finance. *Stress means you're moving up in the world.*

The management team had shrunk considerably so there was no one around to pick up work in my absence. "No one is irreplaceable," said my boss on the day he left, a warning that I could be nudged out next.

In the finance meeting, I nodded and looked interested, mimicking the actions of a woman in control. A woman who deserved to be there. A jumble of numbers and letters, spreadsheets and purchasing software filled the computer screen, signalling more information that I would have to retain in my dwindling brain space.

"Does this all make sense to you?" he asked, eyebrows raised with an air of expectation. There wouldn't be any more training, I needed to understand now.

"Absolutely!" I screeched, a little too enthusiastically.

Instead of going straight to my office, I veered through the shop and checked on a new staff member who was struggling with cashing up their till, then up to the café where I grabbed a sandwich from the counter and took a few bites before getting a debrief on the day from one of the supervisors. When I looked at my watch it was almost five o'clock, another day done and I still hadn't finished those reports.

I took my sandwich into the bathroom and cried.

REFLECTIVE JOURNALING PROMPTS

- *Does your work and personal life feel balanced?*
- *When was the last time you spent quality time with friends and family?*
- *How easy is it for you to switch off from work?*
- *Is work impacting your eating or sleeping habits?*
- *Is work making it difficult to relax?*
- *Does your personal life take a back seat to your professional life?*
- *Do colleagues express concern about your level of job dedication?*
- *Do you struggle to find meaning outside of your work life?*
- *Can you pinpoint any time in the day that is dedicated to you, not work?*
- *How can you increase that time over the next week?*

REFLECTIVE JOURNALING PROMPTS

CHAPTER FIVE

Lack of sleep. That's what I blamed my tears on. If I'd had a car instead of taking the lengthy two-bus journey to work, then I'd have been able to spend longer in bed which would have solved all my problems. This was it, I thought, the final piece of the puzzle. But there was only one problem; I couldn't drive.

In my defence, moving away for university aged 17 meant I had been too young to learn; then when we lived in Glasgow the transport links were really dependable, plus the parking permits were expensive. Learning to drive had never been a necessity, but now it felt as though my life depended on it. So, I started taking lessons.

In the beginning, it was easy to make mistakes and brush them off because I was still a newbie. But a few months in I noticed that I couldn't process what the instructor was saying to me. His lips were moving, I could hear the words, but it was impossible to turn that language into actions. My brain and body felt disconnected in a way that was too scary to admit out loud, so I continued to show up and muddle through.

One evening as I rested my palms on the leathery steering wheel and pressed my feet on the pedals below, I heard the echo of my instructor's voice. It was muffled, like he was shouting at me under water. Quickly his tone escalated, loud and clear now, bellowing in my ear, his hands gripping mine, steering us toward the pavement.

"Do you know what you've done wrong?" His voice was remarkably calm considering I had just driven on the wrong side of the road, straight into oncoming traffic. There was no explanation to offer, no reason for my madness. I didn't trust myself to get behind a wheel after that.

There are moments in life when you realize that things are slipping. When the world tips on its axis and you lose all sense of direction, when things roll out of reach and you're forced to cling onto any available surface with your bare hands.

I tried to compartmentalize these moments into small spaces. A bedroom. A bathroom. Locking the door to maintain the illusion of security.

On the day that things slipped completely, I didn't see it coming.

I was just avoiding another meeting that I didn't feel smart enough to attend.

Hiding from a staff member who asked me a difficult question.

Drowning out the sound of a phone incessantly ringing.

CHAPTER FIVE

Or maybe it was none of the above. Maybe my feet realized before my brain, that today was the last day of pushing.

The glitter on the bathroom floor was pretty. Why hadn't I noticed it before?

Now wasn't the time for looking at the floor. Come on, I egged myself on. Stand up and go back to work. Pull yourself together. Sitting in here was failure, but by forcing myself to sit at my desk and wear a mask ... was that success? Who was the person who wore this pencil skirt? Who spoke about profit margins and staff retention? What was she playing at?

The girl who behaved this way wasn't me; she was a twisted, gnarly version who had a chip on her shoulder and no hope for the future. Her brain was disconnected, sparks flying and smoke emanating from the mains. The communication between my real self and the girl in the mirror had completely broken down. That was the break for me. The breaking down of the person I was. There was no theatrical element, no visible damage to my body, no crumbling in front of an audience, no panic attack in a crowded room. There was just a private, weary moment of acknowledgement, alone in a bathroom, that the pain had become too much to bear. I no longer felt connected to myself, to this job, to this life. Something had to change. That's what I admitted to myself on the day I cried in the bathroom and started Googling the symptoms of depression.

And there they were. Written in plain English for anyone to see. Words like *hopeless, tearful, irritable* and *sadness* hit me like a hammer on the head, driving me deeper and deeper into the hole I was stuck in. No coming out. Why hadn't I looked at them before? Maybe I'd been too scared about what I would find, maybe I'd known all along that there was something seriously wrong with my brain, and I'd known what that would mean for my picture-perfect life. I mentally flipped through memories from the last few years: the angry outburst in my last job, the constant agitation, the sleepless nights, and the more recent, more serious driving incident ... the evidence was in front of me. Undeniable.

When the tears had dried and my mascara turned to crusty blobs, I didn't bother to wipe them away but, instead, limped out of the bathroom and across to my office where I picked up my phone and made an appointment with my doctor.

The next day, I found myself sitting in my doctor's surgery. Just as I arrived, a woman, maybe a few years older than me, struggled to get out of her chair. Two men assisted her as she groaned, breathed deeply, and used every ounce of strength in her frail body to go from sitting to standing. She was hunched over and

SIGNS OF DEPRESSION

There are a number of mental, physical and social symptoms associated with depression and everyone's experience is unique. If you're feeling low, it's important to connect with yourself instead of ignoring the warning signs:

- Low mood for longer than two weeks
- Feeling of hopelessness
- Lack of energy and/or motivation
- No interest in things you once enjoyed
- Thoughts of suicide or self-harm
- Irritability
- Feeling tearful
- Body aches
- Changes in eating and sleeping habits
- Loss of libido
- Avoiding socializing with friends and family

If you consistently experience symptoms of depression for longer than two weeks, seek medical advice.

using two sticks to move from where she stood to the private room, which couldn't have been more than ten feet from where she'd been sitting. She crept slowly, so slowly in fact that the doctor himself came out to see why his next patient hadn't entered his room yet. The whole thing probably took ten minutes, and while I looked on nervously from the other side of the waiting room, all I could think was I'm not that sick. I shouldn't be here.

Earlier that morning, I'd been pacing round the kitchen convincing myself that there was nothing wrong with me. Everyone gets stressed, I told myself. Stop being melodramatic. I was so wound up about asking for help that I had to write down what I wanted to say to the doctor in case I forgot. I scribbled down all my symptoms on the back of a receipt and read them back to myself:

Can't do anything on my to-do list
Worried about something but I don't know what
Tired
Can't sleep
Feel like I'm spinning plates
Crying all the time
Can't cope, can't go on

As the broken woman finally entered the room for her appointment, I felt like an imposter. The only real problem was my failure to cope with the complexity of adult life. I needed to learn how to manage my time more effectively, prioritize and delegate more. I needed to give up my weekends, I told myself, and start committing to the job if I wanted to be successful. Wasting a doctor's time wasn't going to help the situation.

CHAPTER FIVE

Abandoning the appointment was the best way out of this. I should apologize to the receptionist and get on the next bus back to the office. But just as I was psyching myself up to leave, I heard my name announced over the speaker and although my brain was telling me to run, I entered the room and saw the doctor. I started crying before I could utter a word.

I handed her my crumpled old receipt and said, "I need help."

Part One Takeaways

- *Don't disregard the hobbies that you enjoyed when you were younger. Try to reflect on them and actively reconnect with them.*
- *Sometimes your core interests back then are just as prevalent today if you allow yourself to enjoy them.*
- *If you felt pressure to follow a career path that you no longer enjoy, you're not alone.*
- *What you want matters and you should feel able to follow that dream.*
- *Making time to nurture your passions will help you connect with the world around you and maintain a sense of purpose in life.*
- *No job is worth ruining your mental health for. Seek help using the resources section on page 245 of this book.*

PART TWO
PURPOSE

It's a strange thing to admit that having a mental breakdown is the thing that propelled my life into a positive new direction. Of course, I wouldn't wish a mental health crisis on anyone, and on reflection it was perhaps the recovery part of my story that created the conditions for me to reconnect with my passion for writing as opposed to the breakdown itself. In this part, I show you how I found a renewed sense of purpose by using social media and blogging to explore my creativity and connect with a network of like-minded people. Nowadays, most conversations surrounding the internet come with a caveat and this one is no different, so I'm being truthful about the unhealthy aspects of that relationship too. From my self-imposed pressures of living up to an online persona to relying on all the wrong coping mechanisms, this is my warts-and-all story.

The aim is to show you how a sense of purpose can lead to positive changes in your mental health, the ways in which an online connection can be detrimental to this, and how you can be aware of your own behaviours and stay in control. I discuss the pros and cons of networking online when you are socially anxious, the disparity between having online friends and yet still feeling alone, the pressure to live up to external expectations and falling into the comparison trap when mindlessly scrolling. While in some ways being connected online can genuinely boost your mental health, it can also have the opposite effect if you find yourself obsessively checking your device and seeking validation through likes and comments. As well as helping you navigate this part of life, I also show how exploring new career options and finding the one that suits your needs can enhance mental health and wellbeing.

CHAPTER SIX

I'd like to say that the doctor prescribed antidepressants, hugged me and everything was OK again, but that's not what happened at all. What followed was a series of layers, peeling back one by one. To reveal what, I wasn't sure of just yet. But the life-changing jolt that my breakdown initiated was only just the beginning of a long process that is still unravelling today.

For starters, I was given a sick note for two weeks citing work-related stress. When I saw those words handwritten on the note, I was relieved. Validation that, yes, I was definitely stressed, it wasn't my imagination. Internally, I was willing to admit that going into the office was becoming unbearable, so having a medical professional give me permission to stay at home and rest was my get out of jail free card. A momentary release. Externally, I didn't want anyone to know that I was quietly crumbling.

As I left the medical centre with the slip in my hand, I made a mental note of all the little things around the house that needed doing. I should clean the windows, mow the lawn and maybe even get around to decluttering my wardrobe. This was my chance to take back control and get on top of things. Two weeks off was going to solve all my problems. I was certain of it.

But when I got back home and closed the door behind me, I kicked off my shoes, threw my jacket on the floor and crawled into bed. The house was left untouched and even though sleeping during the workday felt like a personal failure, I was too tired to resist.

WHAT'S THE DIFFERENCE BETWEEN STRESS AND MENTAL ILLNESS?

Stress is a normal part of everyday life and can help motivate you. A little bit of stress is actually good for you, but when experienced over an extended period of time it can be harmful. Stress is normally related to a specific stressor, whereas mental illness will continue to be present even without a related stressor present. Everyone reacts differently to specific stressors, so it's important not to compare your ability to cope with someone else's. If you're worried about your stress levels, speak to your doctor.

Signs that you are experiencing too much stress include:

- *Feeling hopeless, worried, agitated or irritable*
- *Mood swings*
- *Headaches*
- *Lack of energy*

- *Stomach issues*
- *Muscle tension*
- *Difficulty concentrating and/or making decisions*
- *Changes in eating/sleeping habits*
- *Reliance on alcohol, cigarettes and/or drugs*
- *Avoiding friends, family or socializing in general*

Two weeks later, an old work friend came to visit. Joe was there too, and I sat motionless as they discussed plans for the day. Going for food. Maybe the cinema. I gazed out of the window, staring at the horizon. I didn't care where we went or what we did. Not because I was tired, but because I just truly did not care. Nothing mattered. The ball of anxiety that had been lurking in my stomach for the last few months (or now I was thinking about it, had it been years?) had vanished, but the space that remained was a dark, bottomless well. The emptiness would have scared me if I hadn't felt so completely numb.

The thought of food wasn't interesting. It didn't excite me at all. The cinema sounded like too much effort and I'd probably fall asleep anyway. I was uncomfortable sitting listening to the two of them talk about the different options, like a spare part in the situation. I had no real feelings other than total hopelessness. Was this really what life was like if you didn't go to work every day? Without a job title and a workplace, was this really the person underneath? Would I ever feel anything good ever again?

Their conversation became distant whispers as I slid out of their company and into the bedroom where I wept uncontrollably. Big, industrial-strength sobs that could have woken the neighbours. For the first time ever I considered all the ways that my friends and family would be better off without me. There was no reason for me to continue living, so I systematically thought about the most painless way to die. When the tears overflowed, I found solace in the finality of nothingness.

When my two weeks' sick leave was up I saw my doctor and described how my previous state of fear and agitation had now changed into something far more sinister. She ran through a standard questionnaire about my mood, asking how often I was thinking about harming myself or taking my own life, and whether I relied on drugs and alcohol. She asked if I had made any plans to kill myself? I answered honestly; no, I haven't made any plans. It's just a fantasy because I'm too much of a coward to go through with it. I hung my head in shame.

The doctor nodded in concern and took notes on her computer, then wrote me a prescription for antidepressants. My new sick note – this time for a month – no longer told a story of stress but was stamped with one single handwritten word: depression.

REFLECTIVE JOURNALING PROMPTS

When you feel at your worst, remember that all emotions are temporary. In my experience, the longer you try to resist sadness, the harder it is to avoid.

- What negative thoughts are you having today?
- How are those thoughts showing up in your body? Where can you feel tension, discomfort, agitation?
- What has triggered these negative thoughts?
- Do these negative thoughts serve a purpose?
- Who are you without these negative thoughts?
- Now read back the journal entry and practise observing what you've written as thoughts you've been having. For example, when you read the words "I am worthless" reframe this as "I am having the thought that I am worthless." Do you see how this can help you step outside of your thoughts and separate them from your sense of self? Just because you think you're worthless that doesn't make it your entire being.
- What are the words you need to hear right now to soothe yourself?

My mental breakdown had worn me out to the point of exhaustion and my body needed rest. So, for a long time, I didn't really socialize with anyone because I slept a lot. I was also very, very sad, so I felt like I had nothing positive to say to anyone.

I didn't want to talk to anyone, because I'd spent the last year experiencing sensory overload in terms of social interactions. I had been acting like a girl boss, a role which I was clinging on to desperately but felt unable to fully execute. So I was constantly on high alert, on stage, acting the way I thought I should act, performing the role of confident team leader, sales director, buyer, health and safety expert, or whatever hat I needed to wear at that particular moment.

I was just tired from years of going through the same routine with no room for error. I had been religiously applying my makeup, wearing the appropriate costume, and doing the moves that I thought I had to do to function as a human. There was no doubt in my mind that I needed the rest to recover, but something else happened during the eventual three months I was off work which only served to make my depression harder to deal with.

I had to be away from work to feel mentally better, of course, but being off sick was embarrassing. It was like being stripped of a medal or told that I was of no use to society any more. Ever since I'd been a teenager,

I'd attached things to my personality to demonstrate my worth. When I was a kid, it was my ability to write stories or sing a song, then as a teenager it was my love for band T-shirts and live gigs. When people struck up a conversation with me, I was able to point to these things and show them the outline of who I was. Who I thought I was.

Why get out of bed when you've got nowhere to go?

Why get washed when you'll be staying home?

Why see friends when you've got nothing to say?

Eating in a restaurant felt shameful. Delicious food was to be enjoyed by the useful members of society, to sustain their contributions to the world or as a reward for their hard graft. So, when my friends tried to invite me out for food, I ignored their calls and stayed in bed.

CHAPTER SEVEN

A few months later and the suicidal ideation had become much less frequent as the antidepressants slowly tweaked whatever chemicals were running through my veins. There was still a looming cloud above me, but I reasoned that these feelings of hopelessness couldn't be a result of my job. Because now that I was off work, life felt even harder than before. Perhaps work had been the one thing that had been keeping me going all along? Yeah, I would be tired and sad but at least I'd be useful. I'd have something to distract me from my feelings. I had to go back. I had to try to regain a part of myself. Work was all I had.

For some reason, three months off work felt like it should be enough. Any longer and I assumed people would think I was taking liberties, lounging around and collecting my sick pay, instead of doing a hard day's work. Emphasis on hard.

After a chat with the HR department, we agreed that a phased return would ease me back into my duties, starting with three days a week in the office instead of a full five. On the morning of my first day back, I watched the sun peek through the blinds before my alarm went off. I'd been awake for hours, lying stiff with worry about the day ahead. I wrote it off as harmless nerves and got up, put on a nice dress and told myself all the things I told other people when they got the Sunday night scaries. *It's never as bad as you imagine. Sometimes the thought of it is worse than actually doing it. You'll be fine.*

On the bus I daydreamed about the driver falling asleep at the wheel and crashing into a building or sailing off a cliff. That would be the end of it.

It's just one day at work. Stop being so dramatic.

When I arrived at work and entered the building there was something in the air. The walls seemed thicker and uncompromising, edges sharper, potentially lethal. I tried to shake off the feeling of doom and went through the motions of my day. I said hello to the supervisor on shift. I attended the morning meeting. Around 11am, a manager from another department came to my room and asked for my opinion on a range of packaging items that she'd been working on, clearly relieved that I was back and able to sign off on her work so she could steamroll ahead with the project. I nodded politely and agreed to whatever she wanted, and when she left the room I closed the door and cried.

I didn't even bother hiding in the bathroom.

What was the point?

I used to be worried about being found out as an imposter, a failure. But I couldn't pretend any more and I didn't care if it meant losing my job because, truthfully, and I'm not sure I'd admitted it to myself until that day, I hated my job. And if that wasn't a valid reason for crying in public, then I didn't know what was.

The last time I'd been in the office I'd been rushing around doing five things at once, desperate to impress, and set on running my departments to the best of my ability. Time away shed a light on things and I didn't like the way things looked now. My perspective was shifting.

As I sat staring at the sickening yellow wall in my office, crying into my hands and not caring who saw, I concluded that in that moment there was no meaning in my work. None that I could see anyway. There was a soft knock on the door and the head of HR poked her head into view.

Seeing the state I was in, she closed the door and offered me a tissue from her pocket. "It's OK if you need to take some more time off to get yourself well."

She was being so extremely kind and a big part of me hated her for that, for seeing me so clearly, for knowing that I was incapable of coping. I couldn't think of anything to say to defend myself.

"No one should be crying at work," she said sympathetically, which is a rule I think we should all live by.

A few months before I'd knocked on the door of the doctor who started my process of recovery, I was in the work canteen talking to a friend from another department. She did mostly admin, didn't really have any understanding of what it was like to work in customer service and ate the same thing for lunch every day. Cheese sandwich. Apple juice. Two packets of ready salted crisps.

I picked at a bowl of limp salad leaves and tried to think of a way to phrase my disconnection from work.

"It's like I keep working, harder and harder, but I'm never going anywhere." My words didn't accurately represent my experience, another signifier of the widening gap between my internal self and the world around me.

"Right," my friend said, as she shovelled the remainder of her crisp bag into her mouth and crunched, licked her lips and tried to make sense of what I was saying.

I knew she wasn't the best person to be opening up to about this, but she was right here, right now, and a warm rush of hope filled my chest as I waited for her response.

"Why do you always have to be going somewhere?"

Working in a tourist attraction was the last place on earth I wanted to be, but I didn't know how to say that without offending her. She would be in this job until she was made redundant or forcibly removed. A great employee, but static.

"I just kind of hate my job," I said, with a rising intonation that made it sound like a question. Through a mouthful of salty crisps she laughed, spitting crumbs onto the table and said in a rather patronizing way, "Oh darling, everyone hates their job!"

Is that really where we're at? A place where work is a thing to be endured with a stiff upper lip instead of enjoyed with a sense of alignment? We've normalized this unhappiness at work to the point where it's quite startling to witness someone get excited about their job, to talk kindly about colleagues or express gratitude for their time spent in the workplace. I'm not saying that there's a perfect job out there where you'll only come into contact with people you really click with, carry out tasks that deliver endless endorphins and earn a million bucks a minute. Deliriously happy at work isn't necessarily achievable, but that doesn't mean that you have to settle for sad and hopeless. If you feel that there is potential for you to uncover a sense of meaning from work, then you should go exploring.

A few weeks after my failed return to work, I awoke at 3pm and it took two hours to psyche myself up for a wash. My pits stank and my hair was a tangled knot on top of my head; the only real motivation I could find to get in the shower was that I would allow myself to sit down in there if I had to.

Sitting hunched over, letting the water soak into matted hair I tried not to think about who I was becoming. But at the same time, it was all I could think about.

Not working made me feel invisible.

Later, as I lay on the floor wrapped in a towel, my phone buzzed. It was an old friend from university inviting me to a party in Glasgow and for a moment I imagined a future where I put on a nice outfit, got on the bus, went to her flat and had amusing conversations with interesting people. In reality, I knew getting on public transport was only something I could do if I was feeling particularly stable (which I wasn't) and that talking to strangers would only happen if I was in a sociable mood (which I hadn't been for months).

My main worry was being asked, "What do you do?" Well, I wake up in the afternoon and normally spend the first few hours of my day crying uncontrollably. When I've exhausted that option, I fall asleep again until 5pm. When I wake up, I figure that the day is almost over so there's no point in showering, and I don't have the energy anyway. On a good day, I cook an oven pizza, but on a bad day I opt for a plate of cookies and a couple of bottles of red wine. The evening ends with me asleep on the couch or awake until 5am, listening to sad songs, and wondering why I'm even still alive.

When my phone beeped for the second time, I kicked it under the sofa and went upstairs to put on some clean pyjamas. That would be my triumph of the day. Raking through the weeks of laundry on the floor, all I could find were pyjamas that were less dirty than the ones I'd taken off mixed in with all my old work clothes. My favourite pencil skirt, a lilac floral dress that I'd bought in preparation for the warmer weather, a pink cardigan that had stains on the wrist from years of making coffee. I gathered them up into a ball and stuffed them to the back of the wardrobe, too embarrassed to acknowledge what I had lost. From then on, I wore tracksuit bottoms and oversized T-shirts in muted greys and navy blues. In shops, I purchased sale items from the men's section with the aim of hiding my body and blending into the crowd. I was a nobody, I didn't deserve to be seen.

During those six months off, I probably appeared to be having quite a nice time. To the outside world, I was working out daily, getting plenty of sleep, socializing a few times a month, and checking in on Facebook with a witty status update every few days. I wasn't too invested in social media and didn't find it to be a source of anxiety like many young people do when they're going through a rough patch. But I wasn't having a good time at all.

Most weekends I would drink wine until I couldn't see straight. If I was with a friend, we could easily get through five bottles of red wine in a night, then go out to the pub the next day and have a beer to cure our hangovers. The anxiety I felt in social situations had become so unbearable that I simply had to be drunk in order to enter the room. Without that safety buzz, I was frozen, and if someone tried to talk to me, I would often just ignore them or leave the premises entirely. Without a job I was a nobody, and alcohol gave me a personality. One drink inevitably led to another and another, which temporarily eased my feelings of anxiety but had drastic consequences. It would amplify my depression symptoms to painful heights. Sometimes, this would be the day after the drinking session, but often, everything would come crashing down bang in the middle of a night out and I'd barricade myself in the toilets of the pub and have a breakdown.

It all came to a head one night when I got drunk and had a stupid argument with a friend; one that, in hindsight, wasn't very important but also somehow signified a clear fork in the road for my relationship with alcohol. Surrounding myself with party people was not good for my recovery, so I stepped away from the friends who only wanted me when I was drunk and decided that until I felt at least a little bit better, I had to remain sober.

TIPS FOR POST-PANDEMIC SOCIAL ANXIETY

If you're struggling to handle the anxiety of socializing with people after being in lockdown for so long, you're not alone. It's normal to feel apprehensive about navigating social situations after being told to stay isolated. But connecting with others is essential for your wellbeing and can be done at your own pace.

- *Be honest with the people you are meeting and tell them how you are feeling. Sometimes just having someone on your side makes socializing much easier.*
- *Plan your exit and have someone on hand to call if things get too much. Make sure you have your travel pass or money for a taxi in case you need it.*
- *Imagine yourself a year from now and consider whether the thing you're anxious about will matter then.*
- *Journal about the worst possible outcome of going out to socialize, then journal about the best possible outcome. Which one is more likely?*
- *Talk to your doctor. Medication might help to alleviate the physical symptoms of anxiety (sweating, increased heart rate, shaking) enough to give you the confidence to socialize again.*

One of the ways I remained sober was by focusing on exercise and I found that time spent on the treadmill helped me figure out a lot of personal issues. It pains me to admit it, but moving your body is an effective way to temporarily shake off those negative voices and motivate yourself to make change. Something about movement makes anything seem possible. During my darkest periods I found that walking stimulated my creative brain more than anything else, so much so that I also started to feel an itch to create something myself. Going back to work as a manager was off the table, and I wasn't ready to work in any capacity, really, so I continued to think about my future in a purely hypothetical way. Change was on the horizon but still far off in the distance and that was easier to handle. On optimistic days, I started going to the gym for something to do. When I started walking on the treadmill, little hopeful notions began to appear in my field of vision. But whenever I had the odd moment of inspiration to look for a new job, depression spoke loudly in my ear. It seemed to take pleasure in telling me that I was worthless and incapable of holding down a job, as well as laughing at the idea that I could actually change careers and start afresh.

On the bus, I scrolled through job adverts on my phone. Like window shopping for clothes I couldn't afford, I imagined myself in roles that didn't quite

MOVEMENT AND CONNECTION

Before rolling your eyes at the well-known concept of exercise being good for your mental health, look at your habits and be honest with yourself. Are you moving your body regularly? If not, try some gentle stretching as you watch TV or lie in bed. Then try something from this list to boost your connection with yourself:

- *High-intensity exercise can give you an endorphin boost and burn off anxious energy – perfect for when you're stuck in an overthinking loop.*

- *Yoga will slow down the mind and allow your body to relax. When you find particular poses difficult, connect to your inner strength and acknowledge that struggling is part of the learning process.*

- *Go for a walk with a friend. Research suggests that movement like this encourages honest conversations and can strengthen connections.*

- *Go for a walk in nature. Connecting with nature can give you a sense of perspective and help you deal with everyday stress.*

fit. Office manager. Not organized enough. Careers adviser. No career to speak of myself. Visual display expert. Lacking in said expertise.

For now, the purpose of getting better had to be enough. Small goals. Getting dressed, leaving the house, going to the gym, picking up bread and milk.

Just as I was starting to see the positive changes of being sober, I was prescribed a different antidepressant which came with a long list of side effects. First came the drowsiness, then the dizzy spells, increased appetite and night terrors. Determined to stick with the meds, I did some research online to find out more and tried to be grateful that at least I wasn't feeling the uncontrollable nausea that others had experienced. In some cases, the drugs I was taking could result in suicidal thoughts. I knew what that felt like anyway and I was willing to risk it to see if these pills could change my brain chemistry in the long term. The lack of purpose had left me feeling useless, and the more useless I felt the more I spiralled. I was doing everything right; following the doctor's orders, getting sober, resting, but the cloud above my head seemed fixed in place and my future was, in my eyes, endlessly bleak. Connecting with my sense of purpose was impossible when I was caught in this cycle of sadness, shame and self-loathing.

I was still overwhelmed with this intense feeling of inadequacy because I was so reliant on my family for money now that I was unable to work. My parents were helping me out with rent money and even paying for my weekly food shop, which made me feel like the worst person in the world. Joe was working in retail and took the brunt of any extra outgoings such as electricity, council tax and other utility bills. Everyone was more than willing to rally round and give me whatever I needed in order to get better. I knew I needed the financial support, but having to accept it only reaffirmed the voice in my head that was telling me I was a failure.

I knew deep down that I had to do something new but I had no skills other than that of a manager, so who was going to pay me to do anything different?

I thought back to my younger days when I would write stories and sing in my bedroom, dreaming of a life on stage or writing books. I couldn't figure out if I had been naïve to think that those things were possible in the first place, or if adult life had just aggressively knocked them out of me along the way. I was hungry for something but not quite ready to take a bite, so I ignored the pangs.

Spiralling into shame was becoming a habit, so I cut off the notion by spending my time on YouTube, watching vlogs by other people who were out living life a little bit better than I was. Kind faces doing makeup tutorials or morning routines gave me a feeling of life progressing at a gentle pace, even if mine had ground to a halt while my brain recovered.

One girl showcased her latest DIY projects, advice about day-to-day life, recipes and beauty treatments, which helped to keep my days light. When the dark cloud grew heavy, I watched her pick out new prints for her kitchen, put an outfit together or try out a face scrub. In one video, she mentioned that she edited an online magazine and when I clicked through to read it, I scanned the headlines. There were similar lifestyle pieces to the subjects in her videos. Fashion. Beauty. Health. Fitness. On one page, there was a callout for submissions asking for writers to volunteer their time to the magazine. No pay, just for fun.

A glimpse of possibility floated into my consciousness. The medication and months of rest had been quietly doing their job in the background, building up my sense of self-worth and giving me clarity of mind to see how my life could take off in a new direction, if I only just took a chance on myself. I read the website again. *No pay, just for fun.*

To me, that meant no commitment, no obligation, no pressure. I sent off an email asking to be considered for a position as an unpaid contributing writer. What did I have to lose?

THINGS TO REMEMBER WHEN YOU ARE OFF WORK WITH MENTAL ILLNESS

- *It's normal to feel guilty about not being at work or increasing the workload of your colleagues, but the best way you can help them is by taking care of yourself.*

- *Celebrate the small wins you achieve on the bad days, even if it's just that you're breathing, having a glass of water or opening a window to get some fresh air.*

- *Self-soothing is easier when you have a plan. Make a list of the things that make you feel a bit better and try to do one of those things every day.*

- *Being off sick doesn't mean that you have to hide away at home. Exercising, socializing, going on holiday or out for dinner are valid ways to spend your time and part of your recovery.*

- *When people offer you help and support, it's not a failure to accept it.*

- *Just because you're not working right now doesn't mean that you'll never work again.*

- *Sometimes you need to rest before you embark on the next exciting stage of your journey.*

CHAPTER EIGHT

After seeing a marked improvement in my mental health since exercising more, gym life had become a staple part of my routine. Piling my hair into a high ponytail was starting to get in the way of my workouts, so I chopped it into a pixie cut which was shaved at the back to make it easier to maintain. Weight began to drop off my face, revealing a sharp jawline I didn't know was there. My clothes were too big for me now but I only wanted to wear fitness gear, so I bought new leggings and sporty hoodies.

I did spin classes and signed up to run a half marathon. Every week, I totted up the hours triumphantly, pleased to see my days had been taken over by so many activities which burned so many calories. I was becoming increasingly interested in losing weight, so I trialled new crash diets, trying to eat clean and survive on a low-carb diet. I had an iPhone at the time and the obsession of taking photographs of everything I did related to food and exercise was beginning to set in. I especially liked taking pictures of my meals, as a way of tracking my calorie intake and holding myself accountable.

One evening, I showed up for my regular spin class to find the room empty; the instructor had been stuck in traffic. As I turned on my heels to leave, the stand-in instructor, a plump woman with red frizzy hair and a friendly smile waved me over.

"We're going to do a weightlifting class instead. You in?" Without needing an answer, she started setting up a step and bar for me and showing me what to do. Without a valid excuse, I panicked and agreed to stay. Lifting weights was something I'd seen men doing in the gym and they seemed to all congregate in an area where women weren't welcome. I had never been interested or brave enough to set foot in their space.

But this was different.

The music was a mixture of 1990s rock and modern pop, which blasted through the speakers so loudly that it gave me the jolt required to lift the weighted barbell above my head and onto the back of my shoulders to start the routine. Watching my reflection in the mirror was like seeing someone else, a woman who was strong and in control, someone on the brink of something exciting.

With the help of the instructor, I picked up the moves, learning to squat, lunge and deadlift while singing along to the music. Basic shoulder, bicep and tricep moves showed me that I already knew how to use free weights and that I had just as much right as the men in the gym to be lifting. By the end of the hour-long class,

I was drenched in sweat, a glisten that felt earned and a feeling of euphoria that lasted for days.

Soon enough, I found Instagram.

I began sharing my pictures of clean meals, like eggs, spinach, and mushrooms, as well as protein shakes and endless amounts of broccoli. So much broccoli. An obscene amount of broccoli. I used hashtags of the diets I followed like #atkins or #whole30 to let others find my feed, and also to connect with other people who were into the same things as me. I found a lot of other hashtags and began following people who have since become Instagram celebrities with millions of followers. The tag #fitspo – meaning fit inspiration – was just gaining momentum and there were thousands of people using it to show off their washboard abs, bulging biceps and perky bums. Finally, like-minded people to connect with. But more than that: an identity that didn't depend on my job title, something to be proud of that I was in full control of. My body.

The images that hogged my feed every day gave me the motivation to get in an extra workout, lift heavier weights, and, of course, eat less "bad" food and more "good" food. The hashtag wasn't the cause of my obsession, but the picture-perfect planet of Instagram was where it lived and I was being sucked into their world.

I was already fascinated with the control that came with changing my own body through the power of diet and exercise, and Instagram was just adding fuel to an already slowly burning fire. It fed this desire, which seemed to be taking over my world rapidly. Without anything else to fixate on, my aim in life was to be the fittest, thinnest version of myself. I was pushing my limits to see how far I could go and everyone on Instagram seemed to be in the same boat.

Everyone in my online circle was in complete agreement; we go big or go home. We didn't make excuses. We didn't wait until Monday to start a diet; the time was now. We ran through the pain, we did workouts on holiday, and rest days were for the weak. That was my life and I very much portrayed that on Instagram because I thought it made me a better person.

For months, I followed a Paleo diet which consisted only of unprocessed meat and vegetables, limited carbohydrates, and no grains or dairy. I became so sick of eating sweet potatoes that just the thought of them made me gag, and living without sugar on such a demanding workout schedule made me incessantly cranky. This choice to eat only "whole" foods was confirmed by all my "friends" on Instagram who were doing the exact same thing. We shook our heads in dismay at others who thought cereal bars were good for you and that wholemeal bread was a healthy option. We knew better.

Online I was all positive vibes and inspirational quotes, but offline I was still crumbling away underneath the surface. Giving up alcohol meant giving up a much-loved coping mechanism and although I acted like I didn't miss booze, I secretly craved it all the time. Being drunk was a quick way to numb difficult emotions and that was always tempting.

But I knew that just one glass of wine would be a gateway to several bottles, and as much as I was desperate for the temporary release that alcohol offered, I stayed strong. I'd like to say that my resistance was because I was getting mentally stronger and that I could see being sober was helping my recovery. But most of the time, my self-restraint was purely a result of my need to control my calorie intake, all in the name of losing weight.

What I didn't show online was pictures of me standing on the scales multiple times a day, waiting for the number to change and ultimately dictate my mood for the day. When I fell off the wagon on more than one occasion, I didn't reveal that I would scoff a sharing-size bar of Dairy Milk within two minutes of finishing my grocery shopping, throwing the wrapper away on the way home to hide my shame.

REFLECTIVE JOURNALING PROMPTS

Not all coping mechanisms are positive although they are often effective, because they allow you to reduce difficult emotions and maintain a sense of balance. Reflecting on your conscious and subconscious coping mechanisms can allow you to connect to what you need and make adjustments.

- *What behaviours do you associate with stress?*
- *What behaviours do you associate with sadness?*
- *What behaviours do you associate with celebration?*
- *Do any of the behaviours mentioned cause you immediate or long-term harm?*
- *Do any of your friends or family say that your behaviours are problematic? Do you agree or disagree?*
- *How could you get a fresh perspective on your difficult emotions?*
- *Who could you talk to about your difficult emotions?*
- *How could you dig deeper into the root of your difficult emotions?*
- *How can you show yourself some compassion when experiencing difficult emotions?*

I began counting everything that went into my mouth and paid to attend a weekly class where I was weighed in front of the group and praised for losing "X" number of pounds. To guarantee a loss every week I drank slimming tea which was essentially a form of laxative, flushing out my insides at an alarming rate to cheat the scales. I restricted my intake to vegetables throughout the day and kept my dwindling energy levels up by knocking back coffee, energy drinks and copious amounts of sugar-free fizzy drinks, which left me irritable as soon as they started to wear off. But it was all worth it as long as I could achieve a body good enough to be displayed on the internet.

I was measuring out porridge oats one morning when my phone buzzed on the countertop. A notification from my email app lit up the screen, a response from the online magazine I had contacted about becoming an unpaid contributor. She was keen to accept my articles as soon as I was ready. Was I ready?

After a few days of avoidance, I emailed back with a few ideas about fitness and healthy eating. She responded immediately and I got to work, motivated by a renewed sense of purpose. Writing came easy and I tried not to overthink the words as they flowed, and before long I was pitching ideas every week and writing 500-word blog posts in between workouts and meal prep. Seeing them published on the website that

I had read as a fan just a few months before was a real buzz, a new one that filled the long days and made me feel hopeful for the future. The more time I spent writing, the more I began to see how disconnected I felt from my previous job in catering. I'd come tumbling off the corporate freight train and I knew it wasn't in my best interests to try to gather the speed required to board it again. Life was now simpler and slower and it was the only pace I could handle.

The only way to maintain this good run of mental health was to minimize work-related stress, so I made the decision to never go back to my job in management. I handed in my notice to work and applied for benefits. With a supporting letter from my doctor, I was given a small allowance each month and along with financial help from my parents, I was able to make ends meet. There wasn't a routine as such, but I fell into a way of life that felt safe. My days were filled with small tasks that didn't require too much brain power. Hanging out the washing. Sorting the recycling. Walking to the gym.

In my little bubble, my only priority was to take care of myself and although I wasn't always managing to do it consistently, at least I didn't have the pressures of work to distract me.

Sometimes I would get deflated and ignore my writing for weeks at a time, burrowing deep into my own thoughts, feeling inadequate and sad. Depression was still very much present in my daily life and often that became my main focus. I fell back into my groove of sleeping, lifting weights, controlling my food intake and soon I was able to step back into my role as a writer. Even when I wasn't writing, I knew that it was something I would be able to return to again and again.

VOLUNTEERING

In the same way that I used writing for an online publication as a way to reconnect with my creativity, volunteering can help you find a new path while supporting your wellbeing and strengthening social connections. Volunteering can:

- *Boost confidence*
- *Reduce loneliness*
- *Improve future job prospects*
- *Offer a new perspective*
- *Give you a sense of purpose*

After a few months of writing articles for the online lifestyle publication, the founder emailed me and said that she was putting together a page on the website to acknowledge all the writers who were contributing to the magazine. She asked me to write up a blurb about myself, saying that it would be an opportunity to link to my website so that people could read more of *my work* and find out more about me. But there was a problem. I didn't have a website. It hadn't even crossed my mind to start writing my own blog, but after a little bit of Googling I figured that there was no reason why I couldn't start one as they were free and easy to set up.

After a few days of considering it, I bit the bullet and set up my own blog.

Thinking of a name for it was my first task. I knew that it couldn't be my name. Well, it could have been, but it was definitely trendier to come up with a quirky title that expressed something about your personality. Everyone was clearly loving the fact that a life lived online could let you portray yourself in the way you wanted, so using your plain old name, which your parents lovingly gave you at birth, wasn't enough.

I wasn't alone in jumping on this bandwagon either, and all the mega-famous bloggers who rule the marketplace today once had online pseudonyms, which I'm sure they'd rather forget about now. Zoe Sugg was Zoella, Estée LaLonde was Essie Button, and Emma Gannon was Girl Lost in the City. The trend for this form of online dressing up was helpful for me, because I was still living in the hangover of my previous life as a catering manager and I really had no clue who I was or where my life was going.

CHAPTER EIGHT

I considered leaning into the niche of health and fitness and tried to think of some witty alliteration using Fiona and fitness, but I wasn't clever enough to think of anything quite so memorable. After a day of dithering around, I settled on Fiona Likes to Blog, which was simple and to the point and didn't rely on any single subject area.

Which meant that the canvas was blank, ready for me to start creating.

CHAPTER NINE

I had a name for my blog, but now I needed to actually write something. With the house empty and Joe at work, my fingers played air piano above the keyboard of the laptop as I considered the outcome. What music did I want to play? Was my voice ready to say anything at all? This was different to being given a brief from the other website I had been writing for; this was my own space where I could create whatever I wanted.

Not working had left my days wide open, but I filled them with activities that didn't seem that meaningful or interesting to other people. I drafted a blog post about all the things I hated about working in catering, but it felt too negative and I was worried it would be too risky in case future employers ever found it. Remembering my days at university, I tried to write something about music and the albums that I had been listening to recently, but it sounded pretentious and boring. They say you should write what you know, and the main thing in my life was my internal struggle with mental illness, but there was no way I was going to air that dirty laundry in public. It was my shameful secret and I didn't want anyone to know that I was depressed and anxious. Even with all the different bloggers I found online, I never stumbled across anyone talking about mental illness and I certainly wasn't going to start the trend. Even if I had wanted to share my story, I couldn't articulate my situation in words. It just wasn't possible. I wasn't ready, and I wasn't willing. If anything, I was using the world of blogging to distance myself from the subject altogether. Online, I could temporarily shed the skin I was in and try on something new for size, so I wrote about my quest to become fit and healthy, focusing on meal plans and exercise routines, and found comfort in the fact that at least if I couldn't have the perfect brain, perhaps I could build myself the perfect body.

As I sipped my first coffee of the day, I heard the rustle of mail through the letterbox. I sorted through the pile, tossing the junk mail and setting aside the ones addressed to Joe. The last remaining envelope was for me, but as an unemployed person with no social life, I wasn't expecting anything other than a bill. But this was worse than a bill. I was being cut off from my benefits.

There is a psychological theory that proposes most behaviour is rooted in our human needs which are organized in a hierarchy. When basic needs (such as food, water and shelter) are met, other needs higher up the chain (such as friendship, intimacy and self-actualization) can be sought after. Although my mental breakdown was a low point and one that stripped me of the ability to take care of myself, having enough money to afford to live during my recovery phase gave me a sense of safety that met my basic needs. So, during that time, I began to let my mind wander, to daydream about the future life I might have. The career that might fulfil me, the job that I would hop out of bed for, stay up late for, grin and smile and laugh about, and give thanks to the universe for.

When I got the letter notifying me that my benefits were being taken away, my quest for a healthy work-life balance was cut short. How could I make a plan to retrain, get a new job, and explore my creative side, when I had no money coming in? I felt like an idiot for even thinking that it was a possibility – a greedy little brat, a lady of leisure with too much time on her hands. Of course I needed to get back to work. I had been stupid to assume a satisfying work-life was in my future.

I got in touch with Claire, the owner of a little bakery and café where I had worked as a teenager, and asked if she was looking for staff. On the day of our meeting, when I walked into the bakery, I was met by several familiar faces behind the counter. My stomach churned as my mind flashed back to the day I wished that the bus would fly off a cliff and take me with it. The day I tried to return to work but it ended in a flood of tears.

MENTAL HEALTH IN THE WORKPLACE

Advocating for yourself at work is essential, even though having conversations about your mental health might seem scary. The following points are made with UK readers in mind, so remember to check your rights wherever you live.

- *Employers are not allowed to ask about your health during the recruitment process. If you're asked about your mental health before a job offer is made, you do not need to answer and you can report this to the Equality Advisory and Support Service via their website.*

- *If certain aspects of your job are causing you stress, try to talk to your line manager or HR department to ask for support.*

- *Legally, all employers have a "duty of care" to do all they reasonably can to support your health, safety and wellbeing.*

- *You have the right to ask for reasonable adjustments (e.g. different shift pattern, alternative work station, etc.) although they may not be granted.*

- *You may get access to an Employee Assistance Program (EAP), which normally includes a mental health assessment and confidential counselling.*

CHAPTER NINE

When Claire asked me to explain why I was looking for work, I froze. I hadn't planned to talk about my mental breakdown, but being in the dusty little office across from the woman who had given me my first job as a sloppy 17-year-old offered safety, so perhaps I could be honest? Tell her the truth about my struggles? But I wasn't brave enough, or perhaps just not ready, so I muttered something about stress and too much responsibility and she didn't probe any further. It wasn't an interview as such, but I was still proud of myself and relieved when I was offered three shifts a week to ease me in.

It was a simple waitressing job where I spent all day making coffees, taking out food, clearing tables and doing dishes. Working in my hometown had felt scary in the beginning, but soon I found comfort in the fact that my old French teachers came in for lunch on a Friday, and that I was making a cappuccino for the doctor who I used to talk to about period cramps. I quietly slotted into place and did the job efficiently, but I didn't feel as though the business would be drastically affected without me. There was something soothing about knowing my presence was helpful but not essential. I found satisfaction in the service aspect, the act of having a conversation with the locals, lending a sympathetic ear to tired mums and lonely elderly folk. There was a joy in knowing that my efforts weren't lining the pockets of an unknown entity, but supporting a long-running family business and attracting customers to the town, adding to the thriving little economy that was happening around me. If I could sum up my purpose in that job, it was to feel like a valued member of the community. And although I knew it wasn't my dream job or long-term purpose, I felt connected to something bigger than me for the first time in years. There was a focus other than my internal pain and that alone gave me a reason to keep going.

CHAPTER TEN

For years I had a sneaky suspicion that happiness didn't exist. In fact, it wasn't a suspicion at all, it was what I really believed. Fear and dread were my default settings, planted years ago when I curled up in that bathroom stall. Rest and medication acted as a sort of weedkiller for when they became overgrown and unmanageable, but the roots were still buried deep, breeding a certainty that sadness would inevitably crop up and take over everything in its path.

So, when Joe and I got engaged during a weekend break, I couldn't understand why so many people were happy on our behalf. People we'd only just met in a bar bought us drinks and toasted in our honour. When we arrived home, cards, flowers and gifts appeared on our doorstep from family members and friends for weeks after we announced our news online. Being the centre of attention was jarring, and knowing that people were excited for us to tie the knot was a strange sensation. I just couldn't visualize the reality that joy could be mustered up so easily, that happiness was just out there for the taking.

I'd known very early on in our relationship that I would marry Joe, because he was unlike any other man I had met before. He has always been thoughtful, kind and sensitive, but when I was diagnosed with depression, I was astounded by the care and attention he gave me. When I cried for days at a time, he didn't patronize me or ask what I had to be upset about. He never questioned the reason for my sadness or tried to throw solutions at me. He was very accepting of my symptoms and never pushed me to try to get better or go back to work before I was ready. I always knew I loved him, but my admiration for him and his strength of character grew immensely when I was at my lowest because he was always around and always gave me a reason to stay alive.

ANXIETY WHEN SOMETHING POSITIVE HAPPENS

The physical experience of excitement (butterflies, increased heart rate, shallow breathing) is similar to that of anxiety, so it's not uncommon for a positive event to trigger misplaced feelings of fear. It is difficult to shift those physiological symptoms so, instead, remind yourself about the story around those feelings. For example, instead of thinking "I'm worried about tripping over as I walk down the aisle", say to yourself, "I'm excited about seeing my partner looking at me down the aisle."

In the lead up to our wedding in 2015, my anxiety spiked massively. I was prescribed a new medication to cope with the symptoms, but the combination of planning and working while still in recovery from my breakdown took over my life.

My worries about the ever-growing to-do list in my mind would temporarily subside as soon as I hit the gym, so I prioritized that over writing my blog. Between work and wedding planning, I had long stopped writing for the online website I was contributing to and without deadlines there was no motivation to sit down and write. The only people who knew about my blog were Joe, a few close friends and a host of strangers on the internet. No one was expecting me to write so I wasn't letting anyone down. My initial passion for setting up a blog was still burning away in the background, but I wasn't quite ready yet to take the plunge and go public with my website because I was scared. What would people think of me? Would they laugh? Tell me to stop airing my dirty laundry in public? I shelved my creative dreams and shifted lanes to plan the wedding, lose weight to fit into my dress and manage the physical symptoms of anxiety that were becoming a daily occurrence.

When the big day finally arrived, I sipped on black coffee with shaky hands as my hairdresser – the little sister of a friend who I used to write songs with at high school – curled my hair. My makeup artist was my maid of honour's sister, so it was a roomful of women who I'd known growing up. Who I'd said hello to in the playground, sat across from in the canteen, got drunk with down the park and cried with when I felt too fat to go to the school disco. My mum expertly tied up my dress wearing a pair of surgical gloves – "I don't want to get it dirty" – and my dad helped me walk along the cobbled pathway toward the ceremony room, as November drizzle fell through the mist of the Scottish countryside.

Having depressive thoughts firmly implanted in my brain for several years had made me secretly fearful that no one was going to care about our wedding, so when the double doors opened and I walked in to see the faces of 60 of our closest friends and family turned out in their best outfits to create the most joyous rainy Thursday I'd ever witnessed, I was relieved. Engulfed with gratitude. Love radiated from every corner of the room.

After being together for 11 years, Joe and I felt that we'd be there for each other no matter what and that saying "I do" was confirmation of a committed partnership. I always knew that marrying this legend of a human being was what I'd always dreamed of, but I didn't realize that it would make everyone else in our lives ecstatic as well. When we said our vows, we

REFLECTIVE JOURNALING PROMPTS

My wedding day fostered a sense of connection for me because I was surrounded by loved ones and reminded about what really matters. It was a day of celebration and signified hope for the future. You might have similar memories from a particular birthday, family holiday, day out with a friend or even a cosy night in with your pet.

- *Can you write about a moment when you felt loved?*
- *Can you use that moment to consider the things that are important to you?*
- *Who makes you feel loved?*
- *When was the last time you connected with those people?*
- *Can you write a letter to someone you love and give it to them?*
- *Describe all the ways you can show yourself some love.*

laughed constantly. Hilarity seemed like the only way to cope with the sheer intensity of emotion packed into the four walls, so we laughed and laughed until the rings were on our fingers and the music played us back down the aisle, hand in hand.

The ultimate Kodak moment for me occurred when I had a few minutes to myself in between socializing, dancing and trying to stick my false eyelashes back on. For a brief moment, I wasn't talking to anyone or doing anything in particular and I looked up to see what was going on around me.

As I watched the room, something started to unfurl inside me, roots coming loose and preparing to let go. Not because I was married or because I planned to start a family, but because I could see the genuine goodness around me for the first time in what felt like forever. Depression had made me think that the world was just pretending to be happy, that no one could really enjoy anything in life, let alone attending a wedding. I thought happiness was a formality that we all had to go through to fit in socially. An unspoken pretence that we all agreed to partake in. But now I could see that it was possible to care for other people and get joy from their joy. For years, I had forgotten that this kind of selfless feeling of being happy for another person was even possible. Even better than that, I was giving joy to other people in my life just by loving another person. My existence, and maybe even my mental health story, could have a positive impact on the world.

Less than 48 hours later we were in a hotel room in Tenerife. Our honeymoon, a generous gift from my parents, gave us time and space to do nothing. As Joe napped on a shaded sun lounger on the balcony, I lay in bed staring up at the fan that whirred overhead, reflecting on everything that had happened to me since I had been diagnosed with depression over three years previously. The deep, dark, rocky bottom where I had been living in the 12 months after my breakdown was as clear now as it had been back then. It rang in my ears like an echo, taunting me daily so that I had been living in a state of fear.

Fear that I'd stumble back to that place, that I was destined to feel depressed for long periods throughout my life, only managing to claw myself back up to a little ledge where I could recover for a few months at a time. Sadness was a long-term certainty, happiness only fleeting.

I assumed that my fall back into darkness was always going to be inevitable, so I had been living with this sense of expectation that meant I was scared to try anything new just in case I failed. Putting my blog into the world was one of those things. I wanted to share it with the world, but that meant being vulnerable to criticism. All I could think about was my previous failings and how ashamed I was to talk about the fact that I didn't work toward a career in music after my degree, or that I couldn't meet the challenge of continuing in my job as a catering manager. I had found a middle ground where I was making just enough money to survive in a job that made no sense to me, but did I deserve better? I wasn't sure.

I certainly didn't feel qualified to jump into the unknown and make a go of blogging. I wasn't making any money from it and no one was reading it, so what hope did I have?

Later that evening, we sat in the restaurant, plates piled high with food from the buffet. Crispy potatoes smothered in garlic, creamy pasta and local meats and cheese decorated my plate. Afterwards, I ate three desserts. Then fell asleep with all my clothes on, defeated.

The day we returned from our honeymoon I was unpacking my suitcase when I came across a blue bikini. For a split second, I wondered if I'd picked up the wrong luggage at the airport but then I remembered that I had worn a bikini on holiday, something that I would previously never have had the body confidence to do.

I dropped everything and opened my laptop, furiously typing out my thoughts about how the wedding day had jumpstarted a new peace of mind and impacted my relationship with my body. I didn't want to be responsible for making other women feel like they had to lose weight to fit into the world. That was how I had been made to feel and it wasn't pleasant. I wanted to make other people feel accepted, worthy and good in their own skin. I reflected on the wedding day and tried to express how the realization had begun to set in and that the way we look does nothing to reflect the essence of the person who lives inside that body. I was quietly pleased with what I had written and felt like I'd spoken from the heart on something that I was only just realizing I was intensely passionate about. In that flurry of focused writing, everyday worries receded into the corners of my consciousness. Writing zoned me into the present moment with precision and clarity, it made me feel wholly aligned with my purpose. Pure Zen. Nothing else mattered when I was writing, because writing was all that mattered.

I've since discovered that this Zen-like state is called "in the flow", a mental state that occurs when you're so engrossed in a task that you tune in deeply to the act of creativity, so much so that you may lose track of time and be unaware of what is going on in your immediate surroundings. A flow state is comparable to a meditative state and will occur when you are doing an activity that you're skilled at but also challenged by.

When Joe came into the bedroom, I was on the floor in the dark, my legs had gone tingly from sitting down writing for so long. Hours had passed and I'd been so wrapped up in the flow of creativity that I hadn't even noticed that day had turned to night.

Despite all the voices in my head, I published the post at the end of November and even plucked up the courage to share it on my Facebook page. To my surprise, some of my friends not only read the article but went on to share it on their own pages, congratulating me on my honesty. A girl I used to work with commented that she had found it to be a "refreshing" read. Other people said it was "inspiring".

Opening up about my vulnerabilities was not only rewarding for me as a writer, but it was affecting other people in a positive way. I had shared something deeply personal with my friends and family, something that I had kept secret from them for so long, and the world hadn't ended. I was hooked.

REFLECTIVE JOURNALING PROMPTS

Are you struggling to find your calling in life? Spend some time reflecting on these points to connect with your passions. If you can't seem to pinpoint your "thing", talk to friends and family to see what they have observed. Sometimes outsiders can pick up on our habits and interests more accurately, and if nothing else, it might give you some food for thought.

- *If you won the lottery, what job would you do just for enjoyment?*
- *What do your older family members say you loved doing as a child?*
- *What subjects are you naturally good at?*
- *Are you known in your friendship group for being fanatical about something in particular?*
- *What similar themes crop up in the books you read or podcasts you listen to?*
- *Do you prefer working with your body or working with your mind?*
- *What do you value more, time or money?*
- *What activity makes you feel like the best version of yourself?*
- *What's the one thing you can do for hours without getting bored?*
- *How do you want your life to impact others?*

CHAPTER ELEVEN

My iPhone was fast becoming my new best friend. Being more honest in my writing reignited my love for blogging, but the more I wrote the more I craved the attention of readers. I started to believe that without constant promotion on social media, no one would know I existed.

The regular feedback I was receiving was a constant reminder that my words were meaningful to some people and this validation, which I didn't previously need, suddenly felt very important.

I watched the likes, followers and page views on my blog slowly increase, and I felt a whole new sense of satisfaction creep into my psyche. A famous mental health charity approached me and asked me to share my story on their website. After years of working in catering, I'd resigned myself to the idea that I was destined to work in a job I disliked for the rest of my life, but here I was working on something creative – granted, for free – and I was genuinely enjoying the process.

I spent a lot of time plonked in front of a laptop, researching topics, trying out new image editing software, reading up on keywords and SEO, creating calendars with all my future ideas plotted out, scouring websites for interesting stock photos, and figuring out how to fix technical glitches on WordPress.

As I began to dig deeper into the world of blogging, I could see that there were lots of people doing it as a full-time vocation and that there was a wealth of information available on how to make the most of your online space. I was captivated by all the women I spoke to and was honestly very grateful that so many of them were sharing their hints and tips on how to increase the traffic to my blog and potentially make money from it.

Of course, I knew I was unlikely to make millions from my blog, but I got hooked on the idea that maybe my little hobby was more than just a way to express myself and connect with others. Maybe my new online persona wasn't a small segment of my identity, but an opportunity to flourish and grow into the person I was always meant to be? Maybe I was just a better person online than I was in real life?

I continued to spend my mornings, evenings and weekends reading and researching the endless routes of possibilities associated with blogging and dabbled in every potential income stream to see if anything worked. I pitched for paid work and got rejected time and time again, sometimes coming away with the odd free product to soften the blow.

My research and experimentation reminded me that I wasn't quite there yet with regards to page views and followers, so no one wanted to pay for my work yet. Then one afternoon as I was sipping coffee on my break at work, an email popped up from the mental health charity I had written for a few months before.

My article had been read over 10,000 times. Hearing that should have been enough, but it just added fuel to the fire. I could see that there was a value in what I was doing, but I wanted to be bigger, have more impact, and engage more people.

Although I was getting more and more interested in talking about my own personal struggles on the internet, I was surprisingly reluctant to talk about my escapades with the handful of people I worked with. The thought of spilling my guts about how sad I felt, or how anxious I was before the day started, was enough to make me feel sick. When customers or staff asked what I did in the evenings, I told them I went to the gym and spent time with my friends.

Every time I received an email from a stranger saying how much they enjoyed my writing, I would open my mouth to tell someone, but then it suddenly seemed like it didn't hold that much importance in the real world. It didn't matter.

I held on to that energy and instead of opening up about my life online, I decided to keep it where it was;

online. At work, I was a quiet, attentive, seemingly happy waitress who made coffees and sandwiches for a few hours every day. When I got home and logged on, I was making a plan to rack up more followers and more page views, and be a success somehow, despite the fear of being uncovered.

Imposter syndrome had been rife in my early 20s but now I could feel it creeping in again on a weekly basis. When I was at work in the café, I would get a dose of reality. Who did I think I was, spouting about my personal dramas on the internet? Why did I think that anyone cared?

I was certain that my Instagram followers were old school friends who "liked" my photographs sarcastically, and that they all talked about me in secret, laughing at all the stupid things I said online. I feared that I had imagined my very minor success as a blogger, that no one enjoyed my writing, and I was being mocked by all the "real" bloggers who thought it was adorable that I had attempted to break into their industry. Then the anxiety and depression would kick in and I felt inadequate, just like I had when I was at my lowest, all those years before.

Unless I could grow my platform and prove myself, I might as well shut down my social media profiles and delete myself entirely.

REFLECTIVE JOURNALING PROMPTS

When chasing a different way of life or a personal goal, it's only natural to feel an element of self-doubt. Your brain will always err on the side of caution and try to convince you to play safe to avoid failure. But if you continue to reconnect to why you're pursuing this particular path, you can move forward with confidence.

- *How does self-doubt show up for you when you think about your sense of purpose?*
- *Reconnect with why you're doing this. Does it matter what other people think?*
- *Who could you share your passions with, knowing that they will encourage and lift you up?*
- *Who should you avoid talking to about this until you feel more confident?*
- *What's the worst possible outcome if you pursue this goal?*
- *What is the best possible outcome if you pursue this goal?*
- *Write about a time when you lived through a difficult time. How can you draw on those strengths today?*

At first, I thought I had food poisoning. It was just after 7am and I was aboard a train leaving Birmingham, alone, having visited some friends. I've always enjoyed the pleasure of a solo train ride, so when the room started spinning and my eyes rolled back in my head I had no idea I was having a panic attack. Everything went black for a second and my head knocked against the tray table in front, which shocked me back to life as I caught sight of my sweaty cheeks glistening in the reflection of the window.

The adrenaline crash afterwards sent me to sleep and when I woke up in Glasgow four hours later it all felt like a strange dream. But I knew it had been real.

Months later, Joe got the news: "I've been offered the job. It's in Birmingham. Shall we go?"

The role of video producer for a video games company was his dream job. We hugged and celebrated and grinned with excitement, ready to hit the road and have an adventure down south. He too had spent many years in jobs that didn't make him feel good, so it was a joy to watch him ride this wave of success after years of struggling to get anywhere.

With just a few weeks to relocate, I took on the job of packing up our belongings ahead of the move. One day when I was placing books into a cardboard box I stopped, compelled by what I don't know, to look at my hands.

Curious, I thought, how they seem to move of their own accord.

I knew logically that they were part of me and that I was in control but at the same time, I had this hyperreal sensation that I was living outside of my body. I stepped away to look in the mirror and my face looked like it didn't belong to me. Who was she? And how long had I been trapped in her skin?

Pushing on with the packing, I distracted myself until the next day, when I took a walk to the supermarket. The pavement looked normal, but I had a sense that it was ballooning and swelling underfoot; I walked cautiously, as though navigating the uneven floor of a bouncy castle. This unsettled feeling continued and got worse, and I felt more convinced every day that I was inhabiting a foreign body. Loud noises made me feel uneasy and I often felt like people were standing uncomfortably close to me.

I was scared of everything.

Even though my body didn't seem to agree, in general I was over the moon to be making the move and embarking on a new chapter in our lives. I pictured a montage of myself learning to paint, growing herbs on my balcony and writing my first novel, culminating in a *She's All That* movie makeover moment where I removed my glasses and became a new woman in time for the school dance. In reality, I was much closer to the character Elsa in *Frozen*, hiding myself away in fear of the outside world.

In the weeks leading up to the Big Move, this fear lurked under the surface of my consciousness.

I started to avoid eating because swallowing anything, even tea or coffee, led to a scary, choking sensation in my throat. But I did what I did best and quietly ignored the whole thing, hoping it would disappear in due course.

We relocated to Birmingham one weekend in June and the sunshine came out for us and lasted all summer. Being a pasty, ginger Scottish lass it took my body and mind a while to acclimatize to the temperature increase in the Midlands, but it was a welcome change and I kept reminding myself that vitamin D was good for my mental health.

What I didn't expect was how much I would revel in the spare time I had in the period before I found a new job.

I walked around the local area, exploring the cafés and canals, seeking out little spots of greenery in the city. My summer wardrobe normally only saw the light of day when I was abroad, but here, it was in circulation every day. I donned shorts and vests and mini-dresses and sunglasses, and floated around the streets like a tourist, soaking up the energy.

Within a week, I was so inspired that I was writing voraciously.

I crept out of bed once Joe was asleep to empty my endless stream of thoughts into blog posts that just kept on coming. I wrote on the notes app on my phone, on scrap paper, on my laptop, and on the inside of the books that I was reading. This was the most fired up I'd felt in a long time and the creativity was exhilarating.

Instead of overthinking everything that I posted online, I wrote things and posted them instantly, often without spell-checking my work. What was the worst that could happen? This was my online space and I could show off my flaws if I wanted.

With this newfound energy, I went from publishing five blog posts a year to publishing daily content. There seemed to be no end to the ideas that flowed through me, a force of creativity that felt like a gift from the universe, an external entity that I just happened to be lucky enough to catch in my brain that put onto the internet. I knew that it wasn't magic but it seemed that way to me. Writing was my superpower.

Part Two Takeaways

- *You can be surrounded by loved ones and still feel alone. Building genuine connections with people who understand you is a key part of maintaining good mental health.*
- *Traditional work culture doesn't work for everyone. It's OK if you don't fit into the typical picture of success.*
- *What you see online isn't the full picture. Don't get sucked into wanting someone else's life because what you see isn't real.*
- *Not all coping mechanisms are healthy.*
- *Creative expression can help you reclaim your identity and process emotions.*
- *Sometimes it's easier to talk honestly about your mental health to a stranger before you talk to your family.*

PART THREE
COMMUNITY

Although loneliness is a major concern in the modern world, a sense of community can help with so much more than that. In this part I show you why building real-life connections is completely different (although often a natural progression) from online connections and why both are beneficial in their own right. I show you the importance of finding peer support and how sharing your story safely with others can give you confidence in yourself, lead to personal growth and exciting opportunities. I share how I slowly turned my hobby into regular paid writing work and the challenges I faced while trying to juggle this alongside my main job – not least the mindset of shifting from one industry to another – and how, although the validation that came from working as a writer has been positive, it has sometimes verged on addictive.

My aim is to illustrate that you can connect with your passions, follow a new path and build a wonderful support network, but you have to be wary of how easy it can be to fall into repetitive patterns of disconnect. A shiny new career looks great on the outside, but if you are still ignoring your internal red flags, then you could just be covering up old wounds that will seep through and cause you pain again and again.

I want you to see that although your purpose, work and wellbeing are connected to each other, it's your connection with your own needs that should ultimately inform your choices and behaviours. I don't necessarily believe that the perfect work-life balance exists and that's beside the point. Being aware of how your actions and environment impact your wellbeing is enough, and striving for a healthier approach will take you closer to your own unique picture of success. Is the fast-paced, "always-on" culture impacting your ability to take care of yourself? Whether you're spending hours on a new hobby, starting a side hustle or laying the groundwork for a career change, I explain how rest should never be an afterthought and, in almost all cases, how it can help propel you forward to the next stage of your journey.

CHAPTER TWELVE

Twitter was where I began searching for more connections.

Me: Any fellow bloggers in Birmingham?

Bryoney: Me! I just moved here from Dundee, would love to chat.

Elizabeth: Same, I just moved here from London and I don't know anyone.

Suddenly, I'd gone from knowing no one in Birmingham to knowing two people who wanted to talk to me. A wave of anticipation washed over me. Within an hour, another girl called Erica joined the conversation and said she'd moved to the city from New York, and later a girl called Claire chimed in, saying she had just arrived from Manchester and was looking to make some friends too. Before I knew it, I'd set up a WhatsApp group for us and we were planning our first dinner date for the following week.

Holy shit, did I just make real-life plans to engage socially with people I met on the internet? WTF?

On the day of the planned meet-up, I woke at 7am sharp to scrutinize every last item in my wardrobe, spending the entire time questioning why I'd chosen last night of all nights to eat an entire tub of Ben & Jerry's Cookie Dough ice cream.

Lately, I'd been spending so much time blogging that I wasn't working out or eating as well as before. I'd given up dieting after the epiphany on our wedding day, but now all my clothes made me look fat, my hair was an out-of-control frizz ball, and my skin was breaking out in spots at an alarming rate.

I took time out from my self-loathing marathon to have a cup of tea and a nice lie down to contemplate the many ways in which I could cancel the dinner date. I could pretend that I had food poisoning but I hate lying, so I thought maybe I could eat something from the back of the fridge and get real food poisoning instead. While I considered eating an out-of-date yoghurt, I made a fresh brew but got distracted when I remembered a comfy shirt dress that I had stashed in one of my moving bags and dug around to retrieve it. After fishing out the item and trying it on, I returned to my cuppa and took a triumphant sip, knowing I would at least be physically content in my faithful old moth-eaten shirt dress. My tea was now disappointingly lukewarm but somehow it still burned my throat. I paused, then took another gulp to confirm my suspicion. The lump in my throat was back.

Just like before, I chose to ignore it. Not because I didn't want to deal with it (I definitely didn't want to deal with it), but because I finally realized why it had appeared in the first place.

I was anxious. Really anxious.

I had suffered from anxiety for years at this point (racing heart, profuse sweating, inability to form coherent sentences), but this felt like something far larger than all of those things. I finally made the connection that this painful lump was a physical reaction to the stress my mind was under, and to be perfectly honest, I was pissed off.

All my instincts were telling me to stay home and set up camp where it was safe, but I had done what all the books talked about and ignored my fears. Of course I didn't want to go out and make new friends in Birmingham. I was quite happy tucked up in my cocoon at home, staring into my laptop screen, and talking to the people who commented on my blog posts. Wasn't that enough?

I sat in front of the mirror and scraped my hair away from my face in preparation for putting on some makeup. As I rummaged around, digging for a lipstick or an eyeshadow to provide a glimmer of hope, I remembered back to the days when I used to go through the same routine every morning before getting on two buses to the management job that made me cry. My face was always immaculate: eyebrows flawless, cat flick perfectly pointed and lashes curled to make my green eyes pop. I looked at my bare, untouched face in the mirror and for the first time in years, realized that I was not the same person I used to be.

I looked similar but not the same, like when you see a photograph of yourself appear on someone else's Facebook profile. A stolen moment when you were unaware that anyone was taking a photograph, and you were just minding your own business at some party, hoping that no one would look your way or want to talk to you.

The girl staring back at me looked tired – exhausted, actually – from being so anxious all the time, from wondering why the world was such a hard place to be in sometimes and when this rubbish party would finally be over. But, above all, the girl looked lonely, and I thought I should really do something about that before the lump in my throat got too big to ignore.

So, I put my face on.

LIVING WITH LONELINESS

- *Chronic loneliness occurs when you are unable to build meaningful connections with people. It is common to have plenty of friends and family in your life and still crave a more intimate human connection.*

- *Social loneliness refers to the lack of a social network that provides a sense of belonging, companionship and membership of a community.*
- *Emotional loneliness refers to the absence of attachment figures and someone to turn to in our lives.*
- *Loneliness, living alone and poor social connections are as bad for your health as smoking 15 cigarettes a day.*
- *Loneliness with severe depression is associated with early mortality and loneliness is a risk factor for depression in later life.*

It only started to feel real when the cold air hit my face. Not just the impending social interaction with strangers, but everything else too. The four years which had passed since I sat alone in that bathroom cubicle wondering where it had all gone wrong for me. All the nights I'd sat motionless in the dark, staring out of the window as the world slept. The once-promising career which was now merely a speck in my rear-view mirror, an echo that sounded like it had been born within somebody else entirely, because the version of me who had chased that dream wasn't here today. She was absent.

All that remained was a fragile, lonely person who was unsure of what lay ahead, but I decided not to think about that. I was only going to think about now.

So, I walked down the street and looked at my surroundings, taking in all the sights of the city as I traced the route to a pub I'd never been to before. I breathed in the late summer air and looked up, observing the city skyline. The evening sun reflected off apartment windows to form walls of warming pink and lilac clouds as I pounded the pavements. Some buildings were old, some were more modern and a large number were still under construction. I spotted one high-rise office block just a few hundred feet from our flat, in the middle of three busy roads which crossed over to form a triangle, where the vacant shell stood awkwardly, marooned and awaiting completion.

Playing tourist in the busy city acted as the perfect distraction and before I knew it, I had reached my destination. Stifling the urge to run, I waved enthusiastically to a group of women who I somehow knew were on my team. I made my way over and sat down, opened my mouth and by some wondrous miracle, spoke like a self-assured, somewhat normal human being.

We sat there for a few hours, five strangers who had nothing in common other than a love for blogging and a need for company. I found out later that Erica had used blogging as a front, merely a way into a community that appeared to have something to offer. She had come to Birmingham from America and was

TAKING ONLINE FRIENDSHIPS INTO THE OFFLINE WORLD

While making connections online is a common way to meet new people, it's worth employing your own safety measures when meeting face to face in the rare event that they are not who you think they are.

- *Do not give your home address or place of work.*
- *Travel separately to meet, ideally with a trusted friend or family member there to pick you up at a specific time.*
- *Meet in a public place.*
- *Drink responsibly.*
- *Don't leave your food or drinks unattended.*
- *Tell a friend and family your location and the time you expect to be home.*

using every weapon in her armoury to carve out a little space for herself in the UK, and I admired her for that.

I too had found a loophole. Meeting people on the internet was not only rewarding but it was, dare I say it, easy. It made socializing more doable for someone like me, who was constantly ruled by anxious and depressive thoughts. When we left, I hugged them all tight without even asking if that was OK. I totally invaded their personal space, but I needed each and every one of them to know how much I needed this, and that they were now my friends.

It wasn't until I got home that I noticed the lump in my throat had disappeared, and with that, I was convinced the internet was becoming my new home.

CHAPTER THIRTEEN

Living in a new city shook the dust off my bones. The blogging community was active, with lots of free events taking place and plenty of writers keen to meet up, share tips, review restaurants and just generally be sociable. My catering career was far from over, as I needed a job to pay the bills, so I took a waitressing job at a local café that was closed on the weekends, giving me plenty of time to explore the local area with Joe and write as much as I could.

Sharing my words with the wider world began to feel like second nature, but being surrounded by other bloggers made me question if I was doing enough. Talking to other women who had tens of thousands of followers on Instagram was intimidating and made me feel like I had a lot of work to do before I could follow my dreams of making a living from my passion. I was constantly chasing an upward trend, and the buzz that came when I got a few new followers or a spike in website visitors. But as soon as I reached another milestone, I was instantly telling myself that it still wasn't good enough. Some blogging events were only open to people who had over 10,000 followers on Instagram and I only had a few hundred, so I wanted to rise in the ranks and have the statistics to prove it.

The thing I love about blogging is how easily accessible it is. You can sign up for a free account with Blogger or WordPress, fill out a few details, and you're up and running in less than 30 minutes. Anyone can write online without paying a penny, which is part of the reason I was able to start doing it at all. I had no income to pay for a website, but I did have an internet connection and the time to write, and that's all I needed. The downside, of course, is that anyone with a blog can offer advice on blogging, but not every person dishing out advice is successful at what they do and it can be easy to fall into the trap of sensational headlines which promise the world.

Even though my mental health wasn't at breaking point just yet, these gurus were unwittingly (or maybe not) preying on my vulnerable side, the side of me that felt unworthy without a bunch of figures that I could recite in order to make my side hustle seem good enough. I'm not too proud to admit that I spent hours reading through blog posts with titles such as *Use this one trick to get more Instagram followers* and *Here's how to make $5,000 from your website in 30 days*. The sceptical part of my brain was telling me that it was all too good to be true, but the remnants of my breakdown had left me weak and in need of regular positive reinforcement to feel like I was succeeding in life.

I'd become accustomed to the buzz of seeing my followers slowly creep up and reading lovely comments on my feed, and I was hungry for more of that engagement even if it was superficial. Not every comment was genuine and not every follower was real. There are millions of bot accounts around and, although I've never purchased followers, I'm sure some of them are lurking on my list until they are next deleted by Instagram.

Every single morning before I went to the café, I would get up at 6am to work on my blog. Sharing content on Twitter, writing Instagram captions, uploading things to Pinterest. I was doing it in some sort of trance every morning while my eyes were still stuck together with sleep and I hadn't had my first caffeine injection yet. When I finished work at 2.30pm, I marched straight home and to the same routine; this time a little more alert and with more coffee in my system.

I was losing so much sleep that I had been downing at least five coffees a day and it was having very little effect on me. I've always been sensitive to caffeine, a curse not only because I love it but because I spent most of my adult life working in cafés where I had unlimited access to the stuff. Normally, more than one coffee made me feel nervous and twitchy, but now I needed several just to shake off the tiredness I was feeling every day. At work, I was knocking back two black coffees before 10am, then having at least two more before lunch. The afternoons were busy so I often only had time for one more, and if I was feeling particularly lethargic, I would treat myself to one of those cans of Monster Energy drinks that are as big as your head.

HOW TO FIND BALANCE WHEN YOU START A SIDE HUSTLE

The ability to start an online business using just a laptop and/or your phone is exhilarating. But in order to avoid it taking over your life, think wisely about how you use your time. Just because you could be using every spare minute to accelerate your side hustle doesn't necessarily mean that you should.

- Use scheduling platforms (e.g. Planoly, CoSchedule, Buffer) to maintain a social media presence without the need to constantly be online.
- Commit to at least one day a week when you don't work on your main job or side hustle.
- Batch similar tasks (e.g. don't switch between writing blog posts and sales calls all day) to maintain creative flow and boost efficiency.

- To curb overthinking, find a side hustle buddy who you can bounce ideas off.
- If you can, reinvest any profit you make into streamlining your processes.
- Make your bedroom a non-work zone and prioritize sleep.
- Track all your wins (no matter how small) so that you can measure your progress over time.
- Work in short spurts and take regular breaks to be more productive and for your wellbeing.
- Practise saying no, whether that's to overtime at your day job or client jobs that don't feel aligned with your mission. Be brave and regain control of your time.

In some ways, I had come so far. I had new friends in Birmingham, a potential new business – at the least, a very time-consuming hobby – and the confidence to socialize again.

But somehow, just as my passion for life returned, I always seemed to take it too far. I couldn't understand why I always ended up sabotaging my recovery by chasing an unrealistic version of success. My friends Erica and Bryoney were always asking me to meet up for drinks and go for dinner, but I was falling into my old habit of refusing because I would rather stay at home with my nose buried in work than be out socializing with real people.

I hadn't realized it yet, but I'd weaned myself off one problem and on to another.

The intense pressure of working as a manager was no longer an excuse. There were no long hours, mind-numbing paperwork or unreachable financial goals. Leaving that environment had been a lucky escape, yet here I was creating these self-imposed and ever-changing targets of getting more followers, more likes and more views on anything I created. I'd separated myself from the militant world of clean-eating because I knew that I was on a quest to have a perfect body that didn't exist, or at least would run me into the ground as I tried to get close to it. Yet here I was trying to maintain a relentless schedule of researching, writing and posting online, which wasn't far off my obsessive need to document all my food choices and exercise every single day. My brain wasn't willing to take ownership of the situation, but my body soon took charge and I began having panic attacks again.

They always seemed to happen in the café where I worked, early in the morning before I'd even had a sip of coffee. One minute I was chopping a cucumber and the next I was scared to use the knife. I didn't feel in control of my body and I couldn't breathe. My colleagues were understanding and didn't mind when I legged it out of the back door and gulped loudly, trying to swallow large gasps of air to keep myself alive. As I leaned on the crusty old bins trying to dig up the root of another cucumber-induced panic attack, I decided that something had to give. I wasn't willing to go through yet another mental breakdown. I couldn't go down that path again.

I thought back to something my mum had said to me years ago when I first complained of work-related stress: "Maybe you just need a holiday."

Her comment had been well-meaning, but at the time it made me feel small and unimportant. The idea that my deep-rooted psychological problems could be cured with a week abroad was like saying I was exaggerating, getting myself all worked up over nothing. Now, even though I was finding my feet in a new city and gaining momentum with my writing I had to admit that a break sounded nice. Slowing down felt like failure, like if I pressed pause I might never press play again. So, I kept going.

10 tips for new bloggers

1. *Building a space online where you can express yourself is a simple and effective way to explore your creativity. Write about something that fascinates you because you'll never run out of things to talk about.*

2. Working in exchange for free products is fine, but remember you're worth more than the cost of a bag of crisps.
3. Clickbait headlines are the worst. Avoid.
4. Don't hassle popular bloggers by trying to get on their radar. Instead, join forces with other small bloggers and collaborate.
5. If you have a blog, then you're A Blogger. Don't sell yourself short or tell people that you're not a "real" blogger. Own it and be proud of your space on the internet.
6. Don't subtweet about other bloggers. It can get nasty real quick.
7. Being yourself is always more interesting than trying to be the next Tanya Burr. She's amazing, but she's not you.
8. You don't have to have any technical skills or a degree-level qualification in English. Just have fun! Don't worry about making your blog look perfect. Instead, focus on writing original content and worry about the rest later.
9. Use spellcheck.
10. Make an effort to be a part of your local blogging community, because as much fun as it is to converse solely through the use of memes and gifs, there's no substitute for meeting up IRL.

CHAPTER FOURTEEN

I'd found this life hack that allowed me to interact with people from a distance, simply by engaging on Twitter, sending a private message to them from the comfort of my own home. It was a little weird, I suppose, but being a little weird felt easier than having to make friends the old-fashioned way, which I assumed involved trying to approach women in a bar or striking up a conversation with the barista who made my latte in the local Costa. And I wasn't into either of those options. Somehow, the idea of quietly sliding into the DMs of someone who had a friendly profile picture and a few familiar hashtags on their feed felt way less creepy and much more doable for me.

Another perk of this approach: when I messaged people, I knew they would snoop around my blog to find out who I was. Instead of being afraid of this, like I might have been before, I felt open and relaxed. I'd been doing lots of rejigging on my blog – I had a fancy logo and some pretty images, so I felt my website looked as swish as it could for spending zero money on the entire project. I felt like it was a fair reflection of who I was.

I hadn't found the courage to fully address my mental breakdown in detail, but in each blog post, I was peeling back more layers and using words like depression, anxiety and mental health whenever I felt it was appropriate to what I was discussing. Previously, I wouldn't have even considered talking about my depression and anxiety with a friend unless it was completely necessary, and definitely only with people I trusted with my life. Apart from my best friends and family, not many people knew about the depths and detail of my mental illness, and this was a reason why I found socializing so hard in the first place.

I just didn't quite have it all out in the open yet, but it was making an appearance in my little space on the internet and it was there for anyone who wanted to read it. Meeting up with people in real life who already had an awareness of my interest in mental illness was refreshing.

REFLECTIVE JOURNALING PROMPTS

Opening up to people about your personal life, especially your mental health, takes courage. Don't worry if this is something that makes you feel uncomfortable in the beginning; try taking it slowly and writing down how you feel with pen and paper. Writing down things from your perspective can feel empowering and give you a clearer idea of what you want to say when the time eventually comes.

- *Are you hiding parts of yourself from your friends and family?*
- *Who are you trying to protect by bottling things up?*
- *Can you brainstorm ways that you can express yourself safely?*
- *What would you do if you weren't scared of other people's reactions?*
- *How would you like to feel when you open up to friends and family?*
- *What are the benefits of being more open about how you are feeling?*
- *Try writing a letter to people you care about and sharing more about your struggles. You don't have to send it.*

Not only did this ease my anxiety, but it often brought me instantly closer to people who had their own struggles with mental illness. I was using blogging as a way of owning the parts of myself that I had been too ashamed to talk about, and I was connected with people who understood how that felt. It was all a complete accident, really, and I'd only ever been writing as a way of creating something for myself, but now it seemed to be having a small – but tangible – impact on my readers.

In my quest to make more friends via the social media loophole, I became part of a Facebook group for bloggers in my area. I was kind of intrigued to see how many new friends I could make through this platform, almost as a way of proving to myself that it wasn't a fluke.

One particular night, I had turned up to a food tasting in an art gallery and I got talking to a blogger called Sinead. I recognized her from her profile picture, and although I had never read her blog, she was active on Twitter and was always my go-to person for the coolest coffee shop recommendations. I popped over to say hello and we bonded over our previous careers in catering management, although I was still working in a café and she had graduated to a training apprentice assessor.

We began talking about the blogging community and why we'd started writing, but as time passed, we became increasingly irked that no food had yet been brought out. We admitted that we had both avoided eating too much earlier in the day, excited at the prospect of the unlimited free food which we had been promised on the invitation. We planted ourselves near the kitchen door and agreed that we would remain there until the food was brought out to the crowd, as we could sense there may be a scuffle when 40 hungry bloggers battled it out for the belated buffet offering.

I'm not sure if it was my increased self-confidence or simply low blood sugar due to the lack of food, but in my delirious state, I found myself going into immense detail about my mental breakdown to Sinead on our first meeting. The poor girl probably wanted to run for the hills, but she certainly pretended to be incredibly interested, even though she had no personal experience of mental illness nor wanted to hear about mine (or so I told myself the latter).

"My brain just stopped working," I told her, with a smile on my face that I imagine made me appear slightly unhinged.

Sinead maintained eye contact, intent on listening to my story.

"Then one time, I drove on the wrong side of the road and didn't even realize!"

Nodding intensely as I spoke, she stood defiant in her decision to wait out this intense interaction with the promise of some free finger food. After I'd spouted out my life story to Sinead, I was shell-shocked at how much information I had divulged to someone I'd only just met, and how easily too. Our initial introduction felt like we'd been friends for years. Sinead didn't pity me or try to get me to change the subject, but she did thank me for sharing my story and when the food turned up we stood smugly in our prime position and stuffed our faces. Not only that, but Sinead has become a good friend and one of the people who I know will always have my back, especially when it comes to the business of living life online.

Something shifted in my psyche that night. There was a thrill in the moment of cracking myself open and letting everything spill out in front of another human being, a kind human being who genuinely wanted to listen. As I walked out of the gallery, I looked up at the night sky, stars prickling and gleaming, as a reminder that we're all connected by an energy and without openly sharing that energy, stoking it, enveloping ourselves in the fiery warmth of real conversation, who are we?

I had the power to reach the individual through my story. This suddenly felt far more effective than focusing on the number of faceless profiles who clicked on my website.

It was around this time that I started using the Stories feature on Instagram. Before long I was talking to the camera every day, explaining my daily struggles, from finding the strength to be cheery at work to my unpredictable low moods. I wasn't talking to many people. I think I had about 1,000 followers when

WAYS OF SHARING YOUR OWN MENTAL HEALTH STORY

You don't have to go public with your personal experience to build a connection with yourself and others. Here are some more gentle, often private, ways of navigating your mental health battles, while aiming to maintain a connection to what feels right for you:

- *Keep a diary to write down your experience.*
- *Join online support groups with private forums.*
- *Write a song or a poem.*
- *Express yourself visually through photography, painting or collage.*
- *Talk to your doctor or ask to be referred for counselling.*

I started using Stories, but I was having some really meaningful conversations in my private messages with people as a result of these random insights into my depressed and anxious mind. Up until then, I had been using Instagram as a way of picking at my physical flaws and finding ways to change them, but now I could see that there was value in publicly celebrating the parts of life that I used to be ashamed of.

Sharing my bad days online was making me more proactive in my own wellbeing, prompting me to evaluate my mood and take practical steps to improve my situation. Just the simple act of saying, "I feel sad today" out loud to the camera felt like therapy.

Soon, I started to get messages on Instagram from people I knew saying they understood how I felt. I got a message from someone a few years below me at school asking for advice on how to cope with anxiety, and once I'd gotten over the surprise, I actually had some words of wisdom on the subject: limit caffeine, prioritize sleep and get some exercise, I said with an air of authority, while caveating my message with a gentle reminder that I wasn't a medical professional. It turned out that she had already had several conversations with her doctor and wanted to talk to someone else, someone who could supply a different kind of support, a level of empathy that she hadn't experienced in the doctor's office. According to the Mental Health Foundation, peer support like this can improve wellbeing and result in fewer hospital stays as well as develop larger support networks and boost self-esteem, confidence and social skills. I'm not suggesting that you should seek out the support of strangers who appear to have the same struggles as you. Don't assume that people who talk openly about difficult aspects of their lives have the capacity to take on your problems too; in fact, this can be quite triggering. Always ask permission before sharing your personal story with someone else and respect their boundaries if they say they're unable to give you the space to do so. If you'd like to offer support to others, try to be an active listener but never try to diagnose or give them medical advice.

My friend Claire messaged me to tell me that one of her colleagues had come through to her office to tell her about an inspiring article she had just read about body image. She was very smug when it turned out to be one of my blog posts, and was proud to be able to utter the words, "I know her! She's my friend!"

At my brother Colin's wedding, I was approached by one of his friends, who I vaguely remembered from school but had never really had a conversation with. We ended up talking for almost an hour about her personal experience with anxiety. In particular, we spoke about the lump she would get in her throat which made her feel unable to eat, the exact same problem I had experienced just before I moved to Birmingham. One thing I knew for sure was that this conversation would never have come up naturally, but because she had read my blog and followed me on Facebook, she felt like she was free to talk to me about it with ease. It wasn't awkward or weird. It was talking to a friend who just needed to get something off her chest.

I'd kept in touch with Sandra – a boss from a previous job – and she messaged me to say how sorry she was that I had never felt comfortable enough to open up to her about my mental illness. And she wasn't the only one. People I worked with years ago messaged to thank me for sharing my story, while university mates got back in touch to say that they too suffered from depression and anxiety and identified with my issues.

The funny thing was that despite knowing that mental health affects everyone, I was still shocked at the people who came out of the woodwork to tell me about their own troubles. I didn't have the passion to pursue a career in the music industry, but there was one girl on my university course who we all knew was destined for greatness. Never work-shy, she was always the first to volunteer for extracurricular activities, foreign exchange programmes and work experience opportunities. She wasn't a know-it-all or a teacher's pet; she just had a natural talent for business and really knuckled down to get what she wanted. None of us were surprised when she was offered a job with an independent record label and relocated her entire life to London, and if anyone deserved the success it was her. She was confident, calm under pressure and a woman to be reckoned with in the best possible sense.

When she messaged me about her mental health issues, I was taken aback. Even though I had seen the negative impact of a stressful career first-hand, I still partly thought it was my personality type that didn't mesh well with a hectic schedule. I assumed other people thrived under pressure, but I was beginning to realize that mental illness didn't discriminate and took hold of even the strongest of people. There were no medals for pretending to have your shit together.

That evening I phoned my mum, and we booked a holiday.

SELF-CARE STRATEGIES FOR LISTENING TO OTHERS

If you choose to be open about your mental health, you might find that friends, family, even strangers, take this as an invitation to share their own struggles. While these conversations are important, you should remain connected to your own emotional needs first and foremost. Don't risk your own wellbeing to offer support to someone else.

- *Be honest. If you don't have the capacity to fully listen and support someone, then gently signpost them to an alternative option.*
- *Let go of the guilt. You're not responsible for helping others recover just because you empathize with what they are going through. Just listening is a great way to support someone.*
- *Check in with them at a later date, picking a time when you are mentally well and have the energy to talk again.*

CHAPTER FIFTEEN

In the lead up to the holiday, I did all the usual things. I panicked and bought three bikinis, two pairs of sandals, and a dress I was almost certain I wouldn't wear. I got my hair cut and I treated myself to a brand-new razor. I fished out my passport and put it in a poly pocket, then stashed it in the top drawer of the bedside cabinet so that I could look at it every day to make sure it hadn't somehow walked itself out of the door.

A week or so before we were due to leave, I started writing a list of all the boring essential things that I would need to take: a phone charger, plug adaptors, medication, headphones. As I looked down the list, I wondered if I should take my laptop with me. I thought that it would be handy if we wanted to watch a film, although really it calmed my nerves to know that I would be able to respond to emails throughout the week if required.

Then I realized that I hadn't even thought about how this week off would affect my side hustle. I knew I needed some time off, but I hadn't quite figured out that there were still things that would need to be done while I was off. Looking back now, I can see that my idea of what "needed" to be done was quite hilarious ... and wrong.

Sitting down with my suitcase open in front of me, I started drafting a blog post on my laptop. The responses to my writing were giving me so much validation at this point that I didn't want to leave my readers hanging, fearing that if I went offline for a week they would ditch me permanently. I'd been watching my website statistics climb steadily over the last year or so and, although I couldn't compete with big name bloggers, I was proud of the work I'd done and the audience I was slowly nurturing. Stepping back from that progress would be like moving backwards, like failing. Losing that connection with my audience could mean triggering another bout of anxiety or depression. I didn't want to go back there.

When I tried to write up an announcement that I was going offline it just made me sound like a loser. Some part of me must have felt that no one cared about my web presence, that no one would notice my absence.

Pushing my laptop to one side, I opened Instagram instead, and filmed an Instagram Story where I talked about my upcoming holiday. Talking to the camera has always relaxed me, maybe because I was brought up in the age of *Big Brother* where contestants were encouraged to share their deepest thoughts in the diary room. Instagram was my diary room, my space to sound off and vent and share my honest self with another part of the world. To digitally wave to a crowd of people who were most likely feeling the same. I didn't just upload Stories and walk away, I watched them back as a form of self-reflection. In the same way that therapists dig deep into what their clients are saying, I used these videos as a way of analysing my problems from an outsider's perspective. Except sometimes it didn't take much analysing at all, because as soon as the words left my mouth, I found clarity.

In this instance, though, I still couldn't see that I was having irrational feelings about my need to be on some form of social media. I posted my thoughts and continued to feel worried about leaving my blog unattended for a week, concerned that without a digital space I might become irrelevant.

HAVE YOU GOT FOMO?

Fear Of Missing Out is different for everyone, but it centres on the worry of being socially excluded. I was constantly on my smartphone because I wanted to be part of a community where I felt I could be myself. But for you, being on your phone might trigger feelings of sadness when you see other people out socializing while you're tucked up in bed.

Try this:

- Close your eyes and take a few deep breaths. Be present in the here and now.

- *Acknowledge that fear of being excluded is a normal human response, designed to keep you safe.*
- *Remember that you are safe right now.*
- *List three things that you are grateful for in this moment.*

The text from my mum came at 4am. Already awake, I replied saying that I would see her in a minute. I climbed out of bed and got dressed in the dark, wearing the leggings and grey sweater which I had laid out the night before. I unplugged my phone charger and grabbed my toothbrush from the bathroom, kissed Joe goodbye and met my mum in the living room of the flat, where she stood fully dressed with her jacket and shoes on, suitcase by her side.

We were getting an early flight from Birmingham to Menorca, something that I had hoped would calm my anxiety as I'd be up and out of the door before I had time to fully acknowledge the fear of slowing down.

My nerves didn't really set in until we were sitting in our allocated places and putting on our seatbelts. Even with my eyes closed, visions of my first panic attack flashed before me. Beads of sweat prickled along my hairline as the flight attendants did their synchronized routine about exits and life jackets and oxygen masks and whistles.

Engines rumbled, wheels spun, we took to the air and seatbelt lights went off. Levitating over the ocean was a welcome pause compared to the process of gaining momentum or slowing down, so I picked up one of the books I'd brought with me and this served as a good distraction while I tried not to let every little bout of turbulence lead to a full-scale meltdown. Before I realized the time, I was almost a third of the way through Emma Gannon's first book *Ctrl, Alt; Delete: How I Grew Up Online*. Even though I was making a serious (kind of) effort to have a week-long digital detox, reading a book about living online seemed like a fitting way to ease myself into the offline world.

The landing was bumpy, screeching followed by meek applause from some drunk people at the back of the plane. We had landed. All was well.

On a scalding hot bus, it took the best part of an hour to drive through the hilly island of Menorca, and with every stop, we dropped off happy vacationers at their destinations. The longer we sat there, the more I grew to enjoy the swaying motion of the tall coach. Elevator music hummed in the background and as I looked out of the window, the coach gave me a birds-eye view of the peaceful island where I was going to spend the next seven days.

When we arrived at the hotel, we made plans to chill by the pool. While my mum was getting changed, I lay on the bed and plugged my phone into charge. Leafing through the literature on the bedside table, I scanned every page, looking for the password. The magical password.

"Is there no Wi-Fi here?" I asked Mum when she walked back into the room, swimsuit on and floppy hat at the ready. She shrugged in the way that only a Boomer would, utterly unfazed by the prospect of an internet-less vacation.

REFLECTIVE JOURNALING PROMPTS

Fear of Missing Out (FOMO) is often associated with the harmful effects that social media can have on your self-esteem when you see what other people are doing, how others are living their lives while perhaps you feel that yours isn't up to par. These are just thoughts, and ones that can be unpicked and considered against reality. Try these writing prompts:

- *When you fear you are missing out on something because of social media, what emotions come up?*
- *What is at the root of that feeling?*
- *How has this affected your day? Did you feel better or worse before you started thinking about how life could or should be?*

- *What are you grateful for in your life, as it stands in this moment?*
- *Can you write about the facets of your life that don't get shared on social media?*
- *What small task can you focus on right now to make yourself feel good?*
- *Who can you connect with in real life today to boost your mood?*

Clouds peeked into the view of the patio windows and Mum ushered me up from the bed, eager to make the most of the afternoon sun before it gave way to dusk. It was around 4pm and the sun was still relatively high in the sky. It was a warm 26°C so we slapped on a thick layer of sun cream and made our way to the pool, while I held my phone to the sky searching for a connection.

"Look at that," Mum gasped, giving me such a fright I almost dropped my phone.

With a sweeping arm, she gestured at the vast array of empty sun loungers as though they were a treasure trove full of gold coins, "We've got our pick of the lot. It's like having your own private pool!"

We found a spot with a bit of shade, threw our towels down on the baking hot plastic beds, and lay there. Exhaling and dozing, commenting on the cleanliness of the rooms and the colour of the sky. Palm trees that looked like they were straight off a postcard. Ice-cold drinks served with decorative fruit that tasted like it was picked fresh that day.

I lay there and I lay there and all I could think was, I am disconnected from my people and it's driving me insane.

With no alternative, I turned on the data on my phone to check my Instagram, then my blog, then my emails, then Facebook. This loop continued until eventually, I felt the hairs standing up on my arms because the sun had almost disappeared.

I hadn't even noticed.

When we went back to the room to get showered and ready for dinner, I hid my phone under my pillow and went to eat without it. The battery was almost dead from my poolside scrolling and even I knew that checking my social media during a meal wasn't a very polite thing to do. We ate and drank and as the night wore on I became aware of all the times that I reached instinctively for my phone, only to find that of course, I didn't have it with me. After scanning the table for my device 20 times, I stopped counting and admitted that perhaps the distance between my phone and I was a necessary – if a little uncomfortable – process that I was willing to push through in order to fully relax.

CHAPTER FIFTEEN

I needed to have a proper good rest. The kind of rest where you rise invigorated, certain that you must have overslept when, really, you've just had seven hours of quality kip. The kind of morning where you walk slowly from place to place, with no urgency to rush into the day, content with a slow start. Not because you're tired but because you're just experiencing life as it happens, moment by moment.

I'd like to say that we spent the week exploring, took long walks along the coastline, visited museums, and spent our evenings watching the sunset at the beach but that's just not how it went down. The hotel was so quiet and peaceful that we simply couldn't tear ourselves away from the poolside to do anything at all.

It's patronizing to tell people who are anxious and depressed to go on holiday, but in this case, it was just the ticket. Just the dose of blissful relaxation that my mind needed to switch off from mindless scrolling and wake up to what's going on around me.

The best part of the holiday was not necessarily being away from the internet. I love the group of people I talk to on there. I love the freedom it's given me to write about whatever I want. I can tell everyone exactly how I feel and learn something about myself too.

It was the physicality of it all.

Sitting at a table every morning, across from Mum, buttering toast and watching it melt.

PERSPECTIVE SHIFTING

Whether you've fallen down a comparison-riddled rabbit hole on the internet or are just having a particularly anxious day, try these simple hacks to give you a renewed outlook on your situation.

- *Visit a place you've never been before, even if it's just a different bench in your local park.*
- *Write a diary entry as though one year has passed and you've achieved something you're working toward.*
- *Try mentally zooming out from your current situation, looking down on yourself from outer space. Use Google Earth if it helps.*
- *Compliment someone and see how your everyday actions can impact the world.*

Hot sand dusted on bum cheeks, fingers trailing through transparent blue seas.

Cloudy lemonade crackling over clinking ice cubes, toasting to the time well spent.

Living authentically online just doesn't substitute for real-life experiences.

I didn't have any life-changing experiences when I was on holiday in Menorca, but I did have time to do things that brought me pleasure. I got a massage. I let my hair dry in the sun. I ate ice cream for lunch. I read books. In fact, I read so many books that I had to visit the hotel library in the hope that there would be one English book on offer for me to fill up the rest of my week.

One of the best parts of my week was reading *Mad Girl* by Bryony Gordon. I'd never read anything else written by Bryony, and in all honesty, I'd been putting off reading it because I knew it was going to be all about mental illness.

I was worried that it would be too close to the bone, too real, and maybe getting caught up in the details of someone else's illness would even send me spiralling into a relapse.

This couldn't have been further from the truth.

Stepping into her mental health story was like seeing the world through a different pair of eyes. Over the course of a few days, I delved into her world, lived her pain and felt her triumphs, all from the comfort of a sun lounger by the pool. It's a privilege to be able to widen your knowledge with such safety, and one that I had taken for granted. Scrolling through social media was nothing like reading a book, and I was only just realizing how powerfully nuanced memoirs can be, how much empathy and understanding you can gain by immersing yourself in someone else's story. How a book can transform someone's life so quietly, so gently. Reading suddenly felt like the antidote to digital overwhelm, the distraction-free drink of real life, the grounding, the connection with the world that complemented my other ways of connecting with people online. I wondered if I could offer my story in a book and reach people like me, people who needed to see themselves on the page. People who needed to feel seen.

From the very first word to the last, I was gripped by her tale of OCD and depression. Not because it was shocking and dramatic – although it certainly was – but because I understood. The simple act of Bryony – or anyone – writing down the most painful parts of her life in something as permanent as a book was really special to me. It didn't mean that my blog or my Instagram captions weren't important, but it made me realize that they weren't everything.

There were other ways to tell my story.

And there was something so subtly powerful, comforting, and life-affirming about reading *Mad Girl*. After I had finished, I passed it on to my mum and she read it too.

During the pandemic, reading saw a huge boost in popularity. *The Guardian* reported that 2021 saw UK book sales increase to the highest they've been in a decade. But the quality of reading was in question for many, with avid readers saying that they were unable to concentrate due to stress and anxiety, and their usual book choices were not hitting the mark. Feel-good comedy and romance books were on the agenda during lockdown and according to *The Guardian*, fiction sales in 2020 soared by more than £100 million in the UK while audiobook sales increased by more than a third. People had more time to read, but they were also craving escapism, and relaxation. For me, it was all about connection. To induce that meditative state, to slow down my nervous system so that I could listen to my own brain instead of the anxiety brain that was tied to the fear of the unknown.

Mum and I didn't talk in detail about Bryony Gordon's book. But all those times I'd pushed her away when I was depressed, all those conversations I knew we'd never have about our own anxieties, they felt less painful knowing that we had both read the same story and had a better understanding of mental illness. We don't often talk about our emotions, even though depression affects a few other people in my family. But we both read the same book, and we both shared that experience which means the world to me.

Part Three Takeaways

- The internet can help young people explore new identities and find community.
- Use digital connections with caution.
- You deserve to feel happiness at work and feel a sense of job satisfaction.
- Your online identity isn't your real-life identity. If you feel confident online, consider if that translates into real life and if not, why?
- Remember to prioritize connecting with people in real life.
- Rest is never a waste of time.

PART FOUR
YOU

This part of my story shows what is possible when you fully connect with yourself and find your calling. I share my anxieties around switching off from social media, what happened when I tried to level-up my side hustle without disrupting my day job, and my attempt to balance online and offline connections, stay focused on my goals and motivate myself when I had a depression relapse in the first few months of freelancing. I share some hard lessons in asking for help and how I successfully learned to set healthy boundaries in a world where it is possible to work from anywhere, at any time. There is also an epilogue where I bring you up to date on my current post-pandemic state of mind and circumstances, as a reminder that you are always changing, which offers further opportunities for connection to yourself and the people around you.

The aim of this part is to help you turn up the volume on your own inner voice, the one that knows intuitively what you need, the voice of truth, the voice of you. In the face of uncertainty, your internal compass is constant. It's easy to dream of a more meaningful future, but if you're not fully experiencing the here and now then you will struggle to create a life that feels connected to your personal values.

By the end of this part I hope you will feel more connected to yourself and begin to see the ripple effects of that strength on your potential future.

CHAPTER SIXTEEN

I sat in the tiny little airport in Menorca and sipped on the first soya latte I'd been able to get my hands on in seven days. It was bitter, overly frothy, and far too hot, but the aroma reminded me of home so I knocked it back and enjoyed the buzz. I aimlessly flicked through a trashy magazine which someone had left on the table.

I was bored, impatient and dreading going back to Birmingham.

Feeling part of an online community had been my life raft, the proof that I existed, but now I was realizing that the act of disconnecting from the noise of the internet was just as important. Being separate, alone, quiet ... it had made everything so much clearer. The air felt fresher on my skin, foods tasted more delicious, the colours of life glowed brighter.

In the past, boarding a plane at the end of a holiday would have sent me spiralling into a pit of doom. But as we waited at our gate, watching people panic in the final moments of freedom by purchasing perfume and giant bars of Toblerone, I was calm. I had an inkling, a fuzzy feeling inside, and an idea brewing that this was exactly the kind of emotion I wanted to evoke with my own readers, and that maybe, thanks to blogging my experiences, I'd already scratched the surface.

10 signs you're spending too much time online

1. You buy makeup that looks awful in real life but spectacular in photographs.
2. You have a fake account that you use to comment on your own posts to boost engagement.
3. You'd rather scroll online than talk to your partner.
4. You use the word aesthetic when talking about your trousers.
5. You have photographic evidence of every oat milk latte you've purchased in the last six months.
6. You're considering building a home studio for your selfies.
7. Whenever you embarrass yourself in real life you think "this will make a good tweet".
8. You've paid someone to rewrite your Instagram bio.
9. You worry that people will recognize you from your Instagram pictures.
10. You worry that people won't recognize you from your Instagram pictures.

As the cabin crew announced we'd soon be arriving in Birmingham, I unplugged my headphones and waited for the bumpy landing. I thought about my break in the sun and I could already feel the positive effects evaporate into the clouds as I began to think about how much work I had to do upon my descent into the digital world.

I looked down at my phone and wondered if I could keep it in flight mode for a few more days, prolonging my radio silence just a little longer until I figured out exactly what my next steps were.

Crammed into an aluminium sardine tin speeding through the sky, the cold, hard air-con blasting the back of my neck, I thought that maybe, just maybe, I wasn't quite as important as I had once imagined.

I'd spent the past few months in a creative rut, and my depression and anxiety symptoms were creeping back in. A week of relaxation only highlighted that my sleeping habits were the worst they'd been in years: my reliance on caffeine was ridiculous, my muscles were so physically tense that I was getting shooting pains up and down my legs when I tried to sleep at night.

My mind had been suffering for years but now my body was giving me signals too, and the writing I was producing as a result of my tireless efforts was good, but it wasn't my best.

I was hooked up, wired in and spitting out regurgitated content like a carefully programmed machine, following the paint-by-numbers rules of blogging, and hastily pinning up my image for the world to behold without checking what it looked like.

It wasn't really my work at all.

I'd been copying everyone else's homework and only now did I realize how unfulfilling that had become. I'd been sucked into the worst part of the internet's "how to" culture and blindly followed every piece of advice on how to get the most likes, followers and page views possible. Clickbait headlines, sponsored posts and affiliate links had become more important than good-quality writing, and that was not OK.

First of all, I concluded that people didn't even notice when I was offline, because they were – rightly so – all too busy getting on with their lives. And, more importantly, it had proven to me that being disconnected from a world where numbers equal success actually gave me a new lease of life. If being online had given me the confidence to talk about my mental illness, then being offline had given me the space to find inspiration about how to effectively tell my story. Not that I think my story is particularly groundbreaking or noteworthy. In fact, I believe quite the opposite and that's where I find the power in telling it.

CHAPTER SIXTEEN

My story is for the people who are struggling to come to terms with their own thoughts, while aiming to portray an unrealistic existence online. It's for the people who wanted one thing and now want something different, something better. It's for the people who feel like failure is a full stop when really, it's just a comma. There is more to come.

People expect me to share my tips on digital detoxing, but I'm not going to because I don't believe it's a realistic goal for the majority of us. In the same way that crash diets fulfil a need for speedy weight loss, going cold turkey with social media might work in the short-term, but it doesn't address the fact that most people need to learn to use social media in a balanced, sensible way, adopting new habits instead of cutting themselves off completely.

My experience of the online world has its benefits, I am certain of that. The friends I've made, the space to share my writing, the job opportunities. Gratitude is justified for all those things, I just needed to get better at reaping the benefits of the internet and setting limits on my usage. Learning to step away when I reached the tipping point before things got messy.

A few weeks later, I took off on foot, walking up the Birmingham canals. Instead of putting my headphones in, I left them at home, picked up a coffee and sat on a bench. Deep breaths, I tried my best to savour the

REFLECTIVE JOURNALING PROMPTS

Being connected to the present moment can help you tune into what makes you feel good. When you figure that out, you might want to start making plans to do more of what you love. If the concept of goal setting sounds too rigid or like work, substitute this for a gentler "intention setting" and use these questions to point you in the right direction:

- *What goal(s) could you be working toward?*
- *What goal(s) do you feel you should be working toward?*
- *What goal(s) do you want to be working toward?*
- *What's holding you back right now?*
- *What are you excited about right now?*
- *How do you feel right now?*
- *How would you like to feel?*
- *What actions can you take that will take you closer to feeling that way?*

scent of roasted cocoa beans, caramelized and slightly fruity. I waited patiently for it to cool down so that I could take a sip. I took in the fallen fuchsia-coloured flowers scattered on the ground beside me. A flock of geese glided soundlessly in the water. The sun warmed my skin.

Without the time and energy needed to constantly keep up with chasing more followers and page views, I was open, able to breathe and free to say yes.

I stopped waking up an hour early to post on social media.

I accepted that Twitter was never going to be my favourite place to hang out and stopped wasting time trying to think of something witty to say.

I stopped writing clickbait headlines on my blog.

I stopped researching hashtags, SEO and how to make money through sponsored posts.

I stopped checking my website traffic every day.

I began putting my phone on flight mode for 30 minutes at a time to be uncontactable for a while.

I began reaching out to people I knew on Instagram to meet up for coffee.

I began journaling to listen to my inner voice.

I began dreaming about writing a book.

I let go of numbers entirely and something amazing happened; I created more brain capacity. It was like I'd finally decluttered my overflowing kitchen drawer and thrown out all the useless utensils, leaving a clean, vacant storage space just waiting to be filled with brand-new things.

Working in the café was starting to give me itchy feet. I wanted so much to be a model employee, to be chatty with every customer, to put elbow grease into all of it. But my mind had already left the building.

My return from holiday had refocused my energy and I was consistently answering callouts for writing jobs, sending cold emails to small businesses and had even written some online content for a video production company in Glasgow. Paid writing gigs were trickling through and generating a small income, but nowhere near enough to justify leaving catering to pursue a full-time job in writing.

The people I met on the blogging scene were mostly hobbyists, which I respected, but I was starting to feel like maybe I didn't fit in as much as I had previously believed. The restaurant invitations were flattering when they appeared in my inbox, but truthfully they didn't feel like fun anymore. Free food was nice, but I was chasing something different; I'd rather be in bed writing. Ambition put me in a separate category, one that meant I was eager to get paid for my words because it could lead to a career upgrade.

One evening when I was scrolling through Twitter, a blogger tagged me in a post from *Metro Online* who was looking for mental health writers. She said I'd be perfect for the freelance gig.

Tossing the phone to one side, I ran to the bathroom. Pacing the tiles, I tried to busy myself, taking off my makeup and listing all the reasons why I shouldn't send an email asking to be considered.

I don't have an English degree.

I don't have a journalism qualification.

I make embarrassing typos.

My brain wandered, imagining what it might feel like to compose an email to express my interest. My throat tightened, I went lightheaded and leaned on the sink for support. Turning off the light, I said goodnight to Joe and crept into bed, certain that I wouldn't be able to handle the pressure of putting myself out there professionally.

The next day at work, I found myself in a foul mood. Each customer seemed more awkward than the last and the scent of bacon fat clung to my hair as I tried to ignore the glowing neon sign that hung in the back of my mind. *Send the email.*

My heart was begging for a more meaningful future, for a platform to share my mental health story and connect with people who didn't feel represented in mainstream media. The universe was handing me an opportunity and I was letting the fear of rejection get in the way.

On my break, I made a cup of herbal tea and scrolled through the *Metro* website. I browsed the most popular topics and thought about how I could put my personal spin on them. Ideas came to me quicker than I had anticipated, the thrill of creativity flowing through my veins, forming headlines, then opening paragraphs and follow-up stories. I brainstormed ideas that took the opposite stance to the most talked about mental health topics, noted down common misconceptions that the general public has about people with depression, the lesser-known symptoms of anxiety that I wish more people had warned me about. Before long I whittled down my list to three stories that I was keen to pitch to the *Metro*. On my phone, I practised writing a short email and included these ideas, with a link to my blog to show examples of my work. I saved it in my drafts folder, willing myself to forget about it, and went back to work.

The afternoon was busier than expected, with a nearby office placing an order for a huge sandwich platter at the last minute. I was up to my ears in tuna mayonnaise and salad dressing for hours, trying to stay positive as the energy drained out of me. When, finally, all the sandwiches were prepped and sent out for delivery, I escaped to the bathroom before embarking on my closedown checklist. Another late finish, another day working on things that didn't feel right.

I grabbed my phone from my pocket and opened up the email from my drafts folder and read the words back to myself, scanning for typos. I took a deep breath and before I could change my mind, I hit send.

CHAPTER SEVENTEEN

"You can't go on like this," Joe whispered in the dark. My feet throbbed under the bedsheets and my hands tingled with anxious energy.

He was right, but I didn't want to admit it. My temporary blogging stint with the video production company in Glasgow had become a regular gig, giving me the chance to write lots more content for the business and manage their social media presence. It paid a few hundred pounds a month, which was a huge financial boost and ego-boost to my freelance business. Before long, more opportunities started to pop up in my inbox. Writing for other websites, small start-up businesses and freelancers who wanted to outsource copywriting tasks.

The thing about having a side hustle is that it's a constant balancing act. I was spinning plates: literal ones in my day job and figurative ones in my personal life. Being paid to write was incredible. Finally, the years that damaged my mental health through pretending to be able to cope in hospitality could be behind me, for good.

My mornings were spent in the café making food, washing pots and sweeping floors. The afternoons and evenings were a whirlwind of tapping on keys, proofreading, invoicing and throwing together a meal before going back to my laptop to complete unfinished jobs.

Slouched on the sofa in our flat, episodes of *The Office* played on a loop as Joe laughed and looked over at me for a reaction. He wanted to share moments of happiness with me, but more often than not I was too busy writing to get the joke which, quite rightly, frustrated him.

Determined to make it work, I looked at my bank statements to see if I could work fewer hours in the café. Doing four days instead of five would ease my workload, give me a full day to dedicate to writing and free up the evenings and weekends to spend quality time with Joe. The promise of a looser schedule was tempting, but I had no idea if my boss would go for it because café work doesn't offer flexitime. You can't catch up on serving customers another day or cram it all in just before midnight.

On the day in question, I traipsed around the basement floor of the café, loading up drinks and confectionery into a basket. As I lugged it upstairs to restock the shelves the boss locked the front door and the other employees untied their aprons, putting on jackets, ready to leave. Pine-scented disinfectant filled the air, the signal that it was the end of the working day.

Slowly, I stacked the shelves. Putting off the inevitable, dreading the conversation I planned to instigate.

Waving, my colleagues filtered out of the exit, confirming start times for tomorrow and gossiping about the evening ahead. When the door slammed shut, a gust of wind tunnelled through the shop, sending a chill down my neck.

My boss at the time was the kindest, friendliest man who incidentally lived in the same building as Joe and me. A few months previously, I had been bed-bound with a recurring back injury and he came over to the flat to lend me his massage chair. I sat in it for weeks as I tapped out writing projects at the dining table, not yet smart enough to realize that I needed a proper desk and office chair to avoid writer's neck.

The fear of asking to reduce my hours wasn't about confrontation. It was rooted in the suspicion that I had failed to handle everything on my to-do list, that I was incapable of multitasking, of reaching peak productivity, of being a good wife, a good employee, a good freelancer, a good ... anything.

The sadness I felt just after I was diagnosed with depression sat heavily on my mind, a reminder of how bad things could get if I didn't manage my time correctly. Would asking to work less trigger a relapse? Deepen my sense of inadequacy? I was scared to find out.

I rushed downstairs to grab my things, set on escaping the café without asking my boss anything. Putting it off until tomorrow, or next week. It didn't have to be today.

When I emerged from the basement, my boss was waiting for me.

"You OK?" he asked, buffing the glass cabinet with a paper towel.

A memory flashed before my eyes. The teacher from primary school who told me I could be anything I wanted to be. Who taught me that people are contradictions, that careers can be mixed up and multifaceted. The little child inside of me remembered the hope, the possibilities, the promise of dreams coming true.

Before I could change my mind, I blurted out my question.

"Could I work less?" I asked, holding back the tears that were prickling behind my eyes, "Maybe drop a day? Or have shorter hours?"

He made a quiet choking sound as he coughed, then processed my request, cogs turning behind his eyes, mentally rearranging start times and shifts in his mind.

"Hmmmm," he pondered as I tried to think of how to retract my request, terrified that I might lose my job altogether. "You've got to make time for your writing,

I know that's important to you. I think we could make that work."

Dabbing at my eyes, my shoulders relaxed, the tension of the moment finally released.

"Thank you," I said. "You've no idea how much this means to me."

We agreed that a Tuesday would be my day off, but that I would be flexible to help out with extra hours when other people were on holiday. As I walked home in the late afternoon, the possibilities stretched out in front of me.

The pressure to work myself to the edge of burnout hadn't won this time. I'd spoken up, asked for what I needed and got it. The secret? Being connected to my own needs and desires; being connected to my voice and feeling able to use it.

On my first Tuesday off, I awoke feeling like a kid in a sweetie shop. I didn't know what to do first. Cook a special breakfast of eggs and bacon? Brew a pot of coffee? The library wasn't far away. Would I get more work done in the silence? In the end I wore pyjamas all day and worked from the dining room table like I always did, writing blog posts for various clients, and social media content for another.

The next day I went back to the café, my creative cup topped up and my positive energy filtering out to staff and customers. Days making cappuccinos and toasties

HOW TO HAVE A DIFFICULT CONVERSATION WITH YOUR BOSS

If the idea of having a serious conversation with an authority figure makes you feel anxious, just know that some of the discomfort you feel can be mitigated by planning ahead and getting appropriate support. I've never been keen to talk to my employers about my hours or the impact on my mental health, but in the end sometimes the hardest conversations are the most important ones to have. Try these tips:

- If you anticipate being treated unfairly, ask for someone else to be present (e.g. a colleague or a member of Human Resources).

- Check your emotions before you enter the conversation and if you feel unstable, postpone the conversation until you feel calmer.

- Write down a list of the things you need to say so that you don't forget.

- Be prepared to genuinely listen to what your boss has to say.

- See things from your employer's perspective and offer words of empathy if you feel able.

- Be realistic about your desired outcome and consider if a compromise would serve as a resolution.

felt filled with a renewed sense of purpose now. It was all moving me one step closer to the future.

If I had been walking down an endless road that went nowhere before, this was a swift turn. I was heading in the right direction and taking pitstops along the way. Working in the café was just a pitstop, I was happier than I expected to come back to those days in the café and switch my brain off from the demands of freelancing into something else entirely. And it still offered that much-needed connection to real life that gave me perspective for my writing.

As the weeks progressed, I fell into a routine. Café, writing, café. Watching movies with Joe in the evenings. Walking into town on the weekends. Seeing friends for coffee. It all started to feel rather enjoyable.

Freelance writing jobs slid into my life at a satisfying pace. Just as I was sending copy off to a client, a new opportunity would crop up in my field of vision. With fewer hours spent at the café, I had the time and energy to stay up to date on social media without letting it overwhelm me, which meant more meaningful connections with other writers, small businesses and potential clients. Some of the projects I took on weren't my area of interest, but I relished the chance to broaden my skill set, finding pleasure in adapting a fashion press release into a blog post or researching interior design tips to form into digestible social media content.

As I found my groove I began to wonder if I was doing it all wrong, because for as long as I could remember, work had been something to complain about. *Nothing good comes easy*, read the quote in every CEO's corner office, so what was this laidback writerly life that I'd stumbled into? Every few days I searched for full-time writer vacancies, egged on by my inner critic who told me that a bustling office and a monthly salary was the only way to establish myself, to build on this momentum. The voice in my head was saying "stop coasting" because I always thought that coasting was a bad thing, but this felt joyous, like riding downhill on a bicycle, wind in my hair, sun on my back.

Then my colleagues started to need time off. Holidays. Appointments. Suddenly, I was covering for Karen when she needed to take her cat to the vet and Tim when his brother needed a lift to the hospital. The money that came from doing extra shifts combined with my freelance income was a welcome bonus. Money to invest in new software, online courses and more coffee that helped me write for longer. Juggling the overtime was doable.

Until I received the email. The email I had tried to put out of my consciousness, knowing full well that it was lingering – an unanswered question.

I clicked it open and scanned the words in front of me. Then again. I read it a third time to confirm that I hadn't misread the sentences and constructed my own truth.

The communities editor of the *Metro* had read the story ideas I'd sent over. She liked them, one in particular, and asked if I would be free to write it up and send it over as soon as possible.

CHAPTER EIGHTEEN

Mornings have always been hard for me. There's no deep and meaningful reason for it; I just love sleep and when I first wake up I'm grief-stricken at being torn from my blissful slumber. Sleep is when my whirring brain turns off, and as someone with anxiety it's a much-needed relief from my inner critic.

One Tuesday morning, when I was working from home, I blinked through sleepy eyes to a package from my friend Amy, who I first connected with on Instagram, where she posts about the power of affirmations. When she sent me a message suggesting we collaborate online, I was sceptical. I've always hated the idea of thinking positive – having depression makes it virtually impossible some days – but I was willing to be convinced otherwise, egged on by a few kind voice notes from Amy (who has the dreamiest Welsh accent).

I opened the package and found a blue cardboard box filled with positive affirmations starting with the words "I can".

The card at the top of the deck simply said, *I can be kind to myself.*

My first instinct was to snigger and roll my eyes. Of course I can be kind to myself. I can buy myself a coffee, I can treat myself to a new lipstick, I can listen to my favourite music.

When Amy messaged a few days before, she told me that every card can have a different meaning based on your circumstances, or what kind of mood you're in.

"Mental health is like the weather," she announced on a voice note, "sometimes it's bright and other days it's a weird mixture of showers, sun and storm clouds. You've got to accept that it's unpredictable."

Looking at my watch, I felt the familiar dread of having slept in later than planned, and internally berated myself for not being at my laptop before 9am. Tired, I pulled the covers up to my chin.

The concept of being kind to myself was something I was well aware of. Since experiencing depression and anxiety, self-love was something I preached about regularly on my blog, but if I was honest with myself, did my behaviour really demonstrate my commitment to the cause?

My best friend Nicola was diagnosed with depression and anxiety not long ago and she's the toughest cookie I know. She's not one to open up about her feelings, and even though I basically make a living talking about mental health, I found it quite awkward to approach her about the subject. So, instead of trying to string a sentence together, I decided actions speak louder

REFLECTIVE JOURNALING PROMPTS

We quite often are our own worst critics, to the point where we treat ourselves in ways we would never accept from external forces. Learning to recognize how harsh you are being to yourself is an ongoing process, but one that gets easier over time. Try these prompts to start showing yourself some kindness.

- *How do you feel when people are kind to you?*
- *What's stopping you from being kind to yourself?*
- *How do you want to feel today?*
- *What small thing can you do today to encourage that feeling?*
- *What habit can you instill to feel this way on a regular basis?*
- *Write about the ways that people have demonstrated kindness to you recently.*
- *How would you carry out similar acts of kindness toward yourself?*
- *What could stop you from being kind to yourself from now on?*
- *How can you recognize and overcome that stumbling block?*

than words and I gave her a pack of affirmation cards. She probably thinks – as I did – that positive thinking is a pile of garbage, but one day in the future perhaps she'll be curious and take a look at what's in that little blue box, and she'll think of me, and she'll know that I care deeply for her.

Could I give that gift to myself? Could I create a life that had self-compassion built into my work and personal life?

With my first assignment for the *Metro* due imminently, channelling self-love would have to wait. I was so riddled with nervous energy that it was threatening to ruin my chance at being published in a national newspaper. If I wasn't running to the bathroom for an anxiety poo, I was pacing around the flat trying to decide if the phrase "comatose cantankerous cow" was too much alliteration for a routine opinion piece. Negative thought patterns circled around a similar theme: *you're lucky to have this opportunity, don't screw it up, the luck will run out soon, better enjoy it while it lasts, but don't enjoy it too much because then you won't take it seriously, take it seriously or you'll screw it up, don't screw it up, you idiot …*

I dedicated my week to writing the piece which was about why I have often chosen to keep my mental illness a secret from employers. When people say it's OK not to be OK, they seem to forget that most bosses don't see it that way. "If I'm too sick, I'm an inconvenience." I typed somewhat angrily into a word document, "If I'm not sick enough, then I'm a drama queen. This is the reality of having a mental illness in the workplace."

Being clever or controversial wasn't my aim. I wanted to hold my existence up to the light and let other people take a look, but, more specifically, I wanted other people with mental illness to read my words and know that they weren't selfish or weird or unloveable. My sense of responsibility with this piece was grounded in my awareness that I had been given access to a large readership and that if I didn't mess it up, I might get the chance to write more. To continue to do my small part in breaking down the stigma around mental illness.

With minutes to spare, I submitted the article to my editor.

The next day, I saw my face pictured next to my name. Fiona Thomas.

Underneath, the headline which had been my idea. From my brain. Now in digital print, beside the name of a national news outlet. I stared at the webpage on my phone as I lay in bed, anxiety stirring and then retreating into the edges of my body, metabolizing into something else. Something positive. Pride.

I copied and pasted the link. Shared it on my Twitter account, Instagram Story, personal and business

Facebook pages. Sent it via WhatsApp to my parents, siblings, aunties, uncles, best friends and blogger pals. Wrote an email to my subscribers and embedded the article so they could read it. Everyone. I wanted everyone to know.

I was now pitching stories several times a week and getting enough commissions to add a few hundred pounds to my monthly income. The thrill of seeing my name in print was affirming enough to quieten the critic in my head. Knowing that my words were to a professional standard, so much so that they were being published, spurred me on to keep steering my career away from hospitality and toward something creative.

Christmas was fast approaching so I took on as much writing work as possible to make sure I could buy everyone nice presents and pay for a few nights out once I was back in Scotland for the holidays. I pitched three or four stories at a time, upping my game by conducting interviews with experts and for case studies, while still writing for my blog and other business clients.

One evening I worked into the night, staying up until 2am to finish a piece of work before setting my alarm for a 7am start in the café the next morning. When I arrived at work, the air felt different. The sizzle of bacon in the pan was deafening, chopping of peppers like a sharp incision made close to my ears. When I reached for a loaf of bread, I witnessed my hand float into my field of vision, the thought appearing as it had done years before. This hand wasn't mine, it was just a prop. Out of my control. I later learned that this sense of detachment is often referred to as "depersonalization", a feeling of being outside of your body and observing your actions, thoughts or feelings from a distance. It can be triggered by stress or a traumatic event.

Bass throbbed in my ears, beads of sweat formed on my scalp. With three big strides, I pushed out of the back door and gasped in the winter air, creating a millimetre of space in my chest for me to recover. To gather myself.

I can be kind to myself.

Over the year or so that I'd worked in the café, I'd been more than willing to help out, covering sick days and holidays, staying late to put deliveries away and trudging through snow to get there when public transport stopped others from making it in for their shifts. I'd never fully disclosed my mental health struggles, but people read between the lines and I'm guessing, read my blog too. My boss had said to me on more than one occasion, "If I can do anything to help, just let me know."

Accepting help isn't something that comes naturally to me, but if it could help swerve another bout of depersonalization then I had to try. So, a few days after the panic attack, I asked my boss if I could cut my hours again.

"Four days is still too much," I said as I trembled from the accumulated anxiety, "I need more time to catch up on everything."

When he refused, I held back tears and forced a smile. OK. No worries. I understand.

But I didn't – I didn't understand at all.

I finished my shift and went home, ready to start work on a writing project that needed completing. The words wouldn't come, they piled up in my fingertips, my mouth, unable to transfer themselves onto the page and into anything salvageable. I rested my head in my hands and caught sight of the clock on my laptop screen. It was 2am. How was I back here again? Hadn't I figured this out? I was beginning to worry that I was dealing with an unsolvable puzzle, unable to conjure up more time in the day to squeeze everything in.

The next morning as he was getting ready to leave I explained to Joe what had happened. That my boss had refused my request to work less hours.

"Well, that's it decided then, isn't it?"

The sense of finality was painful, the end of the road, the end of my dream career.

"I mean," he said with confidence as he picked up his car keys and opened the front door to leave, "you'll just have to quit and make a go of your freelance writing business."

The idea of giving up a reliable paycheque in favour of hobby-turned-side-hustle was wild, so wild that I didn't know how to respond to the very notion of it. Joe left for work and I was left alone in the flat to ponder my next steps.

Someone once told me that your underwear is a visible manifestation of how much you care about yourself. That everyone deserves to wear their best pants every day of the week. That decade-old bras are a sign that you're not supporting yourself.

I remembered this theory as I was carefully stepping into underwear so threadbare I had to make a mental note not to wear them to the gym. They were one squat away from being sent to knicker heaven. Just as I was pulling them up, my thumb tore a gaping hole in the waistband. They had finally bitten the dust.

Raking through my drawers for an alternative, my hand brushed against something soft, stuffed in the corner behind a ball of odd socks.

The maroon velvet box was trimmed with gold hardware. Something I hadn't seen for years, something I'd forgotten I even owned. Running my fingers along the opening, I prised it open. Inside, a gleaming medal.

When I graduated, I'd been awarded the commendation prize for my year but because I left after third year and hadn't completed a dissertation, I'd always told myself that receiving this honour was a fluke, a pity prize, and that my time at university had been a failure. That I hadn't really achieved a proper qualification, that I wasn't smart enough or passionate enough to be a successful graduate. But here was the contradiction. The proof that I had been lying to myself all these years. I had accomplished something, only I'd chosen to hide it away in a drawer and pretend like it didn't exist.

External factors are too often the place I find my self-belief. I have to see it packaged up perfectly in a box before I'll consider the reality that maybe I was always good enough, smart enough, worthy enough.

If I was looking for a bridge to lead me over into the next stage of my career, then this was it.

CHAPTER NINETEEN

The café door chimed as a young mum entered with a grinning baby strapped to her chest. I added milk to my coffee and stirred, watching the bubbles form and disappear.

"So, when will you hand in your notice?" my friend asked, unintentionally sending me into a spiral of self-doubt. I needed to look at my savings, figure out how much money it would take to stay afloat each month and cancel as many unnecessary outgoings as possible. I would approach my boss as soon as I was confident I could make a real go of it.

There seemed to be no alternative. Working a day job and a side hustle had been great for a while, but now the writing opportunities were piling up and becoming unbearable. I hadn't told anyone, but over the last few weeks, my hair had started to come out in clumps. Burnout was revealing itself to me and working to my own schedule was going to nip it in the bud, I was certain of it.

"Any day now," I smiled and changed the subject, eager to talk to her about her life, her dreams, her future. Anything to distract me from the fear of uncertainty that was rippling on the horizon.

Later that evening, I confided in Joe about my doubts.

"I'm not ready. It's too risky." I scrubbed at a dirty mug in the kitchen sink and waited for him to agree.

"But what are the pros of working for yourself?"

Rolling my eyes, I pretended to humour him, as though I hadn't been fantasizing about full-time freelance life every waking moment since he mentioned it.

"I could set my own hours, get more sleep, potentially feel less stressed."

Soapy water circled the drain as I tipped the basin upside down and tried not to get excited about the prospect of spending all day, every day in a creative job. It was too good to be true.

"I mean, less stress sounds ideal," he stroked my back, "you need to take care of yourself and you're pushing yourself too hard at the moment."

"But what if I can't earn enough to pay the rent?" There was a real chance that the unpredictable nature of freelancing would negate all the benefits.

To make sense of my financial situation, I picked through all the income I had taken from writing gigs over the last few months. Joe nodded as he scrolled through my online banking statements and compared them to my expenses. I showed him the small pot of savings I had been accruing. "Your hard work has paid off," he said, squeezing my shoulder and bringing me in for a hug. "I'm so proud of you."

The truth was there in the figures. That I had enough in the bank to pay my bills for the next few months, one retainer client who gave me a stable base income, one other regular client who sent me a few pieces of work a month and, now, a contact at the *Metro* who was accepting and paying for my online articles. If I was sensible, and continued to work hard, it looked as though I was in a position to try out freelancing full-time.

At the end of the week, I awoke at 6am for an early shift in the café. Fridays were always busy, with office workers from nearby businesses flooding in for sausage sandwiches to celebrate the imminent weekend. This routine was something I'd come to appreciate as a hospitality worker, because in many ways I was incredibly lucky to work in a café that was closed on Saturdays and Sundays. Would I miss this weekly tradition?

The morning shift passed slower than usual. I buttered bread, spooned fillings, sliced sandwiches and handed them over to familiar faces, all the while trying to ignore the knot that was forming in the pit of my stomach. Colleagues made jokes and talked about last night's TV, but I kept my head down and rehearsed the conversation I was going to have with my boss.

As the final customers filtered out, I washed up and waited for the right moment. As the other team members slid arms into jackets and unfolded bus tickets, I took my boss to one side in the kitchen.

"I'm really sorry to do this," I whispered. All confidence in myself had shrunk inside the shame of letting my employer down, "but I'm going to hand in my notice."

In lieu of handing anything over – I hadn't written a letter, it seemed too formal – I stood and waited, sure that outrage was looming. As an ex-manager I knew exactly what was running through his head at that exact moment – the prospect of advertising the role, conducting interviews and training up a new employee while still running a business. Red flushed to his cheeks and I sensed panic, but it was overridden quickly with a nod of acceptance and two arms reaching out for a hug.

"I knew your writing was going well," he said, "I'm made up for you, I really mean that."

When the team heard us talking, they came over. I was hugged and congratulated. Everyone could see that this was a step in the right direction for me and a path that I had to follow. There was no question about whether it was the right decision.

It felt strikingly similar to the moment I stood taking in the friends and family who surrounded Joe and me on our wedding day. Friends and family have always raised me up, always pushed me forward, and always believed in my abilities long before I've found that belief myself. Never underestimate the impact your support can have on other people.

A month later, I was a full-time freelance writer.

The work was consistent. Writing social media copy for a client in between pitching stories to the *Metro*. I reached out to my audience on Twitter, mining conversations for article ideas and case studies, and conducting interviews over the phone to complement the many pieces I was now producing every week. Finally, I was exploring issues that were close to my heart such as mental health stigma in the workplace, social anxiety and women who chose to live child-free.

During a conversation with a friend, I learned that she was supporting a family member through a recent stillbirth. Having never experienced something so harrowing, I was genuinely surprised by her efforts to memorialize the little boy who had sadly passed away, and the conversations that the family were having in order to keep the memory of him alive, while acknowledging the grieving process. I couldn't stop thinking about this, and how little I knew about how to talk to someone who has lost a child. Stupidly, I had assumed that the safest option would be to avoid the topic altogether and stay positive for their sake.

There needed to be more awareness about how to communicate with grieving parents, but I quickly disregarded the subject matter as "too difficult" for me to handle.

Weeks later, the same friend sent me a photograph of the plaque that has been installed on a park bench in honour of the baby boy, complete with mother looking on with pride.

My mind was made up then, and for months, I pitched the story relentlessly to every publication I could think of. I interviewed a handful of bereaved mothers who were willing to share their experiences and watched them light up as I asked about their children and their life as a grieving parent. Eventually, an editor (who coincidentally, was doing maternity cover at the time) got back to me and said they would love to publish the story. When I saw my article printed in one of the UK's top-selling women's magazines, it was, and continues to be, one of the proudest moments of my writing career. Not because I saw my name in print, but because I felt a deep sense of connection to the mother and child at the heart of the story, to the mental health struggles that millions of women go through every day, and the fact that I could potentially make some of them feel less alone through the words that I had written.

As time went on, my inbox lit up with psychologists who wanted to talk to me about important topics, radio shows who wanted me to comment on specific issues, and enquiries from small business owners asking how to hire me as a writer. No job is better than another, and although my new role came with some financial uncertainty, sitting at home writing on a laptop far outweighed the stable income that hospitality had offered me.

Clients were unreliable of course. About six months into my freelance journey, I was chasing one particular client every day for 12 weeks before he settled a collection of invoices totalling £200. I was counting every penny and had to fight to be paid fairly a lot of the time.

To make life easier, Joe and I decided to move to a smaller flat with cheaper rent. The downside was the initial cost of moving (deposits, cleaning, removal vans) but on paper, it would make financial sense in the long run, so we found a place and started packing. A few days before the move, I hit an emotional wall.

There was no warning. No trigger. Just steadfast hopelessness.

I lay on the sofa staring at the ceiling for what felt like hours, letting the afternoon sun stream in through the window, pulling my pyjama top over my eyes in an attempt to shut out the world. The thought of acknowledging work made me fearful, the idea of writing a complete impossibility.

My phone vibrated on the glass coffee table and I glanced at the message. It was my friend Amy inviting

10 signs that you need some time offline

1. You tried to "pinch to zoom" your old family photo album because you forgot it wasn't digital.

2. Your friends send out the search party if you don't respond to a WhatsApp message within the hour.

3. You break out in a cold sweat when you have to turn your phone off to go into the cinema or get on an aeroplane.

4. Complete strangers DM you if you haven't updated your Instagram Story in the last two hours.

5. If you visit a café or bar without free Wi-Fi, you down your drink and leave without question.

6. You're genuinely enraged when you visit somewhere aesthetically pleasing, but forget to take a photograph to prove you were actually there.

7. You are managing a separate social media account for your pet(s).

8. You look forward to going to the bathroom so that you can scroll through your timeline in peace without seeming rude to others.

9. You are deeply hurt to find out that a woman that you worked with for one shift six years ago has unfriended you on Facebook.

10. You're secretly relieved that some of this book has been presented in listicle form to make it feel less like a book (yawn) and more like a BuzzFeed article.

me to come and stay with her in Wales to celebrate her birthday. The energy required to travel and socialize with strangers wasn't going to appear anytime soon, so I shoved my head into a pillow and let the tears, the shame, flow out of me.

It was the need to pee that forced me to my feet, crawling to the bathroom and rubbing the heels of my hands into my eye sockets. I pressed hard to see if I could still feel pain. The worry of my work sat heavily on my mind but not enough to motivate me to do any.

Joe arrived home and I ate dinner in silence, hoping that the following day would be an improvement, that I would catch up on the work I'd missed and find my mojo again.

When I awoke the next day, it was after 1pm and the sense of dread remained.

Unread emails stacked up in my inbox, obnoxious in their black and bold type, screaming for attention. Two articles lay half-finished on my desktop, sentences hanging in midair. Deadlines grew closer.

On day three of my slump, Joe asked me what I wanted to watch on TV and I started silently weeping.

"I can't," I whispered at the floor.

"You can't what?" he asked gently, putting an arm around me for comfort.

I shrugged, unable to answer the question. Unable to pinpoint the problem, as though I was facing a brick wall but too close to see what the wall was part of; the entire structure made anonymous by the sheer scale of the thing. Undone tasks clouded my vision, I was frozen. Too anxious to act but too depressed to care.

Relapse.

It was something I'd gotten used to over the years, but secretly, I'd hoped that freelancing would solve all my mental health problems. Flexibility, freedom and creative fulfilment had been the goal and now I was stumbling at the first hurdle. What I wanted was finally mine and it felt ... harder than I had imagined. More mentally taxing than I had anticipated.

All my past jobs – being a manager, working in hospitality – they had been the problem, hadn't they? It was the toxic work environment and the unsociably long hours that triggered my mental health dips, wasn't it? But now, just a few weeks into my freelance career, I was faced with the real possibility that perhaps the jobs weren't to blame. Perhaps I was always going to be mentally ill and being self-employed couldn't change that. I was expecting too much. I deserved to be ill.

"I can't ..." I tried to find the words, "I can't eat, wash, go outside ..." I waved at the lilac sky outside that seemed to be taunting me. Everything was hard, everything was off-limits.

"What would you say to someone who was reading your blog?" asked Joe.

I shook my head and continued to look at the ground.

"Come on," he nudged my shoulder.

The image of the affirmation card I pulled a few weeks ago appeared at the edges of my vision. *I can be kind to myself.*

That's the thing about self-compassion. So often, it starts with someone else showing you that you deserve to be loved. You have to get that permission slip from someone you trust before you'll take the action steps to make self-love a tangible thing in your life.

HOW TO SET BOUNDARIES WHEN YOU WORK ONLINE

I learned the hard way that having a freelance business based online could lead to endless working hours without some careful planning. The always "on" culture is stressful and can take its toll on your mental health. Flexible working is a huge plus point of working online, but there is also the temptation to reply to emails as soon as they appear on your device. Here are some things that I learned to maintain boundaries and protect my mental health:

- *Turn off the Wi-Fi.*
- *Have a work phone and a personal phone.*
- *Tell clients how you prefer to be contacted and stipulate this in your terms of service.*

- *Put your office hours and expected reply times as part of your email signature.*
- *Use auto-reply on Instagram.*
- *Write 'no work DMs' in your social media bios.*
- *Create separate work and personal email and social media accounts.*
- *Move real friends to WhatsApp so that you don't have to open social media apps to connect with people.*
- *Create a "Boundaries" highlight and FAQs on your work Instagram page.*
- *Set an autoresponder on email to give an expected wait time, and signpost people to the FAQs section on your website.*

The next day was similar to the period that followed my initial depression diagnosis. I slept in until the afternoon and argued with myself for an hour about whether I could muster up the enthusiasm for a shower. Forget the enthusiasm part, I thought. What would be the kindest thing to do for myself in this moment?

I padded across the bedroom carpet, sat on the edge of the bath, turned on the water, and poured in all my favourite smelling products. How can I be even kinder to myself, I wondered? A big glass of water and a new book accompanied me in a long, hot soak.

A clean towel, my best pyjamas and a soothing playlist became my wins that day and by the time Joe arrived home, I was marginally less sad and able to eat a proper meal.

When I finally gave in and admitted that I could be – and had to be – kind to myself, it didn't happen all at once. It was reminding myself that I deserved a shower first thing in the morning, instead of squeezing it in during my lunch break. It was recognizing that the kindest acts for myself were often much simpler than I had imagined: brushing my teeth, cutting back on caffeine, finally buying some new underwear. I didn't need a spa weekend to take care of my mental health, I needed to prioritize myself as much as possible in any given moment.

After those basics were taken care of, I began to see other ways that I could be kind to myself. I asked my editors if I could extend some of my deadlines while I got my mental health back in shape, something that took a few tries to follow through with. Saying I wasn't coping and that my work was suffering as a result was painful to admit. It triggered all those old feelings that came up when I left university, or when I hid in the toilets at work instead of doing my job. I felt like I was failing back then and I felt like I was failing again now, but I knew that it wasn't the reality of what was happening, because the nonsense your inner critic spouts is never the whole truth. I was going to take care of myself by asking for what I needed.

I was an expert at putting up emotional barriers with those close to me, skilled at shutting out the people who wanted to help me, who wanted to connect with me. Putting up walls was now a way to protect myself, something I could transfer to my work life. I tried hard to set boundaries to keep work out of certain parts of my life, deleting work apps off my phone, setting up an official work email address and making plans at the weekend to stop me from falling into the unhealthy pattern of staring at my laptop instead of living my life. Success at work and prioritizing yourself should not be mutually exclusive. They can coexist. They must.

Work had the potential to get its hooks into me again if I wasn't careful, but this time round I had the power to shield myself. To heal myself.

In the interests of being kind to myself, I tried to think of the things I was succeeding at, even when my mental health wasn't in the best condition.

I was succeeding at changing my life.

I was succeeding at rearranging my priorities.

I was succeeding at slowing down.

Within a week, I was able to open up my laptop and start writing again. Combined with a new level of self-care, more rest and lots of support from my loved ones, I'd figured out that while learning to connect with your work is important, it doesn't really matter unless you're connecting with the most vulnerable version of yourself too. That person needs your care and attention, that person is your number one.

REFLECTIVE JOURNALING PROMPTS

No matter where you are in life, it's important to look back and appreciate how far you've come. Instead of marching ahead to the next milestone, take a moment to reflect on the strength it took to get to this point.

- *When was the last time you celebrated yourself?*
- *What do you need to forgive yourself for?*
- *In what ways have you made yourself proud recently?*
- *What expectations do you need to let go of to create more space for yourself?*
- *What's the most compassionate thing a friend has ever said to you? Can you make that your mantra?*

CHAPTER TWENTY

Everyone immediately made their way to the bar. It was 2am on a Saturday night out in Cardiff – we were all there to celebrate Amy's birthday. When we got to the bar, I turned my back to the group and did a scan of the room, quickly locating the bathroom at the back of the venue. Without a word, I left the group and headed for safety.

My instinct took me there because I was about to have a meltdown and I wasn't about to do it in front of a crowd of people who I'd only just met a few hours ago.

I knew Amy, but only from the internet. After we'd begun chatting every day on Instagram, we swapped phone numbers and planned on doing some creative projects together.

We lived two hours apart, which I guess wasn't too far, but with Amy having two little boys, she couldn't exactly drop everything to come to Birmingham for the day. So, when she invited me to go to Wales to stay with her for the weekend, I knew I had to pluck up the courage to make it happen. I had been so excited to meet her in person.

The train journey had gone smoothly, a far cry from the panic attack I'd had on that train to Glasgow a few years previously, and at the station, I had been greeted by her and her two boys (she jokingly calls them The Chuckle Brothers) who were both under five and adorable.

We spent the day skimming stones on the beach, collecting shells and comparing our finds, competing to see who had found the shiniest piece of treasure.

Later in the evening, there was a gathering in her house where we sipped from glass flutes and ate cheesy crisps and chocolate biscuits. I was introduced to her old school friends and work colleagues, who all asked questions about how we'd met and what I did for a living.

I decided to drink, not because it would make socializing easier, but because I wanted to let my hair down and have a good time. Over the last 12 months, I had been introducing alcohol into my life gradually. A glass of wine here, a cocktail there. I wanted to feel normal again, like I could have a couple of drinks and know when to stop and so far I had been learning to find that balance.

The night had gone well – we'd moved on from her house to a private karaoke room and now to a busy pub in the centre of town – until I realized that I was all out of energy to keep going. So, I did what I did best. I headed to the toilets.

I sat alone in my bathroom stall trying to control my breathing, but all I could feel was a tightness in my chest and sickness rising in my throat. I was tipsy but not enough to warrant throwing up, and I knew that my tense shoulders and back muscles were a sign that this particular wobble wasn't booze-related.

Adrenaline buzzed through my calves, as I tapped my heels on the floor tiles, but instead of feeling happy and joyous, I felt sad. I couldn't cope, and I was going to end up embarrassing myself in front of everyone.

I began replaying the few hours in my mind and picked it apart, questioning every interaction I'd had, and convinced myself that all of Amy's friends hated me. One girl didn't really say hello to me, did she? Another girl took my place in line when we were doing karaoke. Another said that she had really been looking forward to meeting me because she followed me on Instagram. Well, I guess that last one was a really lovely thing to say, but I'd reacted by hiding in the toilet ignoring her and everyone else.

I'd been acting standoffish for the last hour or so, because the alcohol was wearing off and the anxiety and self-doubt were seeping into my field of vision.

Why is she even here, she's not saying anything?

Why did Amy invite her?

She seemed really nice on Instagram, but she's actually really weird. She's so fake.

I was an imposter. Just like I had been years before when I was "pretending" to be a manager, when I was falling apart inside.

I wasn't meeting their expectations and it made me want to vomit.

I sat in the bathroom crying, trying to relieve the pressure by squeezing my fists and punching my legs. After five minutes or so, I tired myself out and the tears dried up. I couldn't sit in there forever. But I couldn't face going back out there and feigning confidence.

I wasn't ready to put on a fake smile and dance the night away when I was so emotionally drained.

I slowly unlocked the stall door and peered outside. The bathroom was empty, so I ventured outside and washed my hands, dabbed my eyes with a tissue and put on some lipstick, which I found in my handbag.

To anyone else, I looked completely normal, especially considering everyone else in the vicinity was at least a little bit drunk and too busy having a good time. I didn't know what to do. A deer caught in the headlights wondering whether to stay still or run for her life.

I was stuck in a bar in an unfamiliar city in the middle of the night. Normally, I'd just go home but I was too far away, and I had no clue how to get back to Amy's house on my own.

We'd taken a 20-minute taxi ride from her house and I couldn't afford to pay for that myself, not to mention dealing with the awkward conversation I'd have to have with the stranger driving the cab.

CHAPTER TWENTY

I couldn't make Amy leave until she was ready because it was her birthday. I was her guest and I didn't want to cut her night short just because I was having a minor meltdown for no apparent reason.

A rowdy hen party came crashing in, taking up so much space that I had no choice but to get out and leave them to it. With no plan of action, I walked back into the main bar where the music was thumping, and I found Amy and her friends on the dance floor. Someone handed me a glass of Prosecco and I took one sip but I knew that consuming more alcohol wasn't going to help. Discreetly, I placed it down on a nearby table that was cluttered with drinks.

I caught Amy's eye and she tottered over to ask me if I was OK. I mumbled something along the lines of, "I'm not feeling well," and she gave me a hug. A firm, warm hug that reminded me of the power of human connection. She introduced me to her friend Rachel, who I'd not actually met yet, and we instantly got to talking about our mental illness while huddled in the corner of the noisy pub.

Rachel told me that she had bipolar disorder and that she felt totally out of place because her medication had caused weight gain. She felt fat and ugly, and I patted her arm to tell her she was gorgeous, because she was wearing a sequinned jacket that was genuinely beautiful, and her hair was so shiny it sparkled under the disco lights.

I told her that I too felt out of place, that I was worried everyone was expecting someone who they'd got to know on Instagram, and they'd been presented with me instead. I felt like a disappointment and she told me that I was talking absolute rubbish.

Within half an hour, I could breathe again.

Has the internet cured me of my affliction? Has depression been washed away by the soothing tapping on keys and the constant validation in the form of likes and comments from strangers online? Well, that's a hard question to answer because I'm not sure I'll ever be cured.

I've had days when I've felt happier than ever, but relapse is always waiting. I can feel amazing for months, and then one day, just like that night in Cardiff, I'll have a blip that sends me spiralling. Sometimes the blip will last a day, but sometimes I'll feel the dark, dull ache of depression for weeks. It will take over my mind to the point where I can't work. I can't walk outside. There is no joy in anything. I'm back to square one all over again and it feels like it's never going to end.

It's because of these consistent bouts of depression that I think I'll always consider myself at least 1 per cent depressed. Not because I'm a pessimist or because I want to wear my illness like a badge of honour, but because it's just a part of me now and that's OK.

I know now that even if I find myself hiding away in a public toilet from time to time, it's not always something to be too concerned about. Whether I'm in there Googling the symptoms of depression or simply reapplying my lipstick, I'll always find my way out in the end.

Part Four Takeaways

- *Social media is not a long-term substitute for real-life connections.*
- *If you're starting a side hustle, remember to maintain a healthy work–life balance, otherwise you can become consumed by your career.*
- *Your social media statistics are not a representation of your success.*
- *Take regular breaks from social media to tune out the noise. Use this time to reconnect with friends, family and your purpose.*
- *You deserve a job that allows you to set healthy boundaries and prioritize self-care.*
- *Self-compassion is possible.*

10 THINGS I'VE LEARNED ABOUT CONNECTION

1. Without physical spaces to express who we are, your identity can be hard to pin down.
2. Your online and offline selves are connected, but they're not the same.
3. Don't let algorithms make all your choices for you. Escape the echo chamber and experience real life as a priority.
4. Texting a friend is better than isolating yourself completely, but don't take hugging them for granted.
5. Meeting up in person is never as nerve-wracking as you think it's going to be.
6. When your pain is too complex to put into words, art can say it for you. Listen to music, watch films, read poetry, take in art that you love.
7. More connections do not mean better. Choose quality over quantity.
8. The concept of home isn't always tangible or reachable. Find home within yourself.
9. When you're stuck in your head, connect to the body instead. Play an instrument, dance, sing, run.
10. Video chats are great, but sitting in real life silence with a loved one is better.

10 THINGS I'VE LEARNED ABOUT CONNECTION

EPILOGUE

I've come to the Scottish Highlands to run away from my feelings and connect with nature. It looks and smells far better than any bathroom I've encountered.

My friend's parents invited me to stay in their converted garage which functions as a cosy space for tourists – mostly climbers who want to tackle Ben Nevis – but I won't be scaling any cliffs. I didn't even want to come in the beginning.

The alternative was to stay in relative comfort, to choose the familiarity of home over the scary unknowns of real life. I guess two years of global suffering will do that to you; it makes you terrified of the exciting parts of life, perhaps because you think you don't deserve them, or maybe because they seem too good to be true.

I drew on my intuition (she's a wise old bird) and ignored the urge to politely decline and, instead, packed a rucksack with some essentials and boarded the train to Fort William where the never-ending hilltops are either dark and looming, or frosted with snow, cut out against a misty sky looking down on the vast, swaying loch below. Where people choose practicality over fashion, with waterproof clothing, walking poles and sun-blocked noses the order of the day.

In the studio apartment where I'm staying, the walls are adorned with prints of stags locking horns and abstract paintings flecked with gold and cobalt blue. Porridge nourishes me as I write, hot tea and coffee warming me when the wind howls through the hills in the evenings. Outside at night-time, I can see stars for the first time in months.

I am grounded here.

In a space that isn't my own, I am truly at home.

Unlocking the door every morning to greet the commanding, mossy mountains is a ritual I look forward to, the open air a reminder that I am always connected to the world around me, even when I don't feel it, even when it seems invisible and perhaps not even worth searching for.

We are always uncovering new ways to find ourselves and I have been just as dazed and confused as everyone else amidst the pandemic.

When I started writing the first version of this book in 2017, I wanted to prove that living in the digital age could be good for your mental health. I believed wholeheartedly that social media could be a positive force because I had experienced the benefits first-hand through the relationships I had built, the work I've done and the person I've grown into. Without access to the internet, so little of that would have been possible. Of course, this came with a huge caveat. That not all is well in internet land and that you should step in with a curious yet cautious mind.

My story reached people who already understood my message. Readers appreciated the idea that internet friends are real friends, that sometimes the digital version of yourself feels more authentic than the one you present to your loved ones. There was a small ripple of validation from the reviews I received and the messages that trickled into my inbox, saying how refreshing it was to see an alternative narrative to the one on the news. To hear that the impact of the internet isn't always representable in a collection of scary statistics.

But it wasn't until 2020 that the ripple grew into a tidal wave, the unavoidable proof that the internet was going to be the everyday tool that gave us a sliver of control. Online education gave our children a version of routine, remote working gave adults something to focus on and the economy something to cling to, TikTok gave us light entertainment and Instagram gave small businesses a way to promote their goods and services. We shifted our lives to a digital space because it was the safest way – the only way – to find meaning and connection while minimizing the risk of transmitting a deadly virus.

In creating a mirror image of my life on social media during that time, I realized that my real life was somewhat lacking.

Like a lot of people, the long days and nights triggered spiralling thoughts around who I am and what I want in life. Hence why I ended up in this cabin in the woods, because if you can't run off and find yourself in the Scottish hills after a global pandemic, when can you?

I'm so done with pretending to be productive, so ready to admit that I'm a human and I need rest to function at work. Once I've finished writing for the day, I'm having an afternoon nap and I don't care who knows it. If giving myself the gift of sleep is lazy, then so be it; I'm lazy and proud of it. We all deserve more naps.

As we try to fall back into place, to fit into the post-pandemic version of normal, we are not the same. We are different people now. We have questions about our existence, about what matters, about how the new world works and how we will fit into that world and without losing ourselves.

Connection with your work, your desires, your needs, your people *is* possible in the digital age.

Whether you had a mental breakdown like I did or you're regrouping after the effects of the pandemic, use that as the fuel to uncover the connection you need.

Did you reconnect with pastimes you used to love as a child? Make time for them as you move into the future. Use the internet as a way to explore the untapped parts of your identity: try out online courses,

YouTube tutorials, start a blog and learn how to play again like you did as a kid. You don't need to start a side hustle but you can, especially if you're already doing that stuff for free anyway. Why not get paid for doing something you love?

For those of you who are still in school and feeling pressurized to pick a career path when you feel lost, know that while this is an important time in your life, it's not your whole life. Your career will be long and winding with many chances to reroute your destination along the way. Enjoy the start of the journey, have fun and focus on the wonder of possibility. Nurture your passions and don't let anyone tell you that they don't matter.

Living through multiple lockdowns was arguably made more bearable by the fact that most people had access to the internet. We threw Zoom parties, FaceTimed relatives, shifted to remote working and kept small businesses afloat by shopping online. But we also lived our lives through a screen which bred comparison and major identity crises for millions of people. Don't let other people's online personas trick you into thinking you want to be like them. While there are lots of aspirational people online, there are also plenty of false gurus who promise to have the answers to all your problems. Only you can figure out what you really want in life, so don't get distracted by the noise of what everyone else is striving for. Stay in your lane.

Forgive yourself if you're still finding your feet in the new world and, of course, make full use of the digital realm to ease that process. Join online community groups, try dating apps, talk to friends on Instagram, but be brave and take that next step. Invite someone out for a coffee. Go to that birthday party. There is no substitute for seeing your mum's smile in real life or hearing a friend talk passionately about their favourite TV show. If your employer is offering space to work in the office, try it. You never know who you'll bump into or what moments of joy you'll experience. The internet cannot save you. Work cannot save you. But people can, and connecting with them is the first step.

Come find me on Instagram @fionalikestoblog and tell me about your life; I'm waiting to hear all about it.

Listen to what you need. External forces will inevitably drown out your internal voice, but it's still there. Be prepared for the ongoing practice of stepping back and tuning in to hear what you need to hear. Self-compassion will always be worth it and is the best way to strengthen your connection to the most important person in your universe. You.

Fiona

March 2022

AUTHOR'S NOTE

Hopefully, by now, you've come to see that the process of "working it out" is just that: a process.

Finding connection, purpose and personal growth is not a science but an art, and one that requires a smorgasbord of learning, patience, listening and reflection. During lockdown I chose to listen, absorbing as much art as I could through films, books, podcasts and music. I became obsessed with honing my craft as a writer, but there is one thing I've always struggled with – endings.

Aristotle famously said that endings must be surprising, yet inevitable.

When I started writing this book, I had been married for almost two years. Joe was the one who read my early blog posts, the one who drove me to the pitch meeting with my publisher, and the one who convinced me that I had the skills to become a freelance writer.

My writing career has afforded me so many privileges that came after this book and therefore haven't been included in much depth in these pages. One of those things is therapy; and having access to that support seemed minor in the beginning. I had no idea how drastically it would strengthen the connection I have with my brain, body and identity.

In 2022, after a year of psychosexual therapy, I came to terms with the fact that I am, and have always been, a lesbian.

Hindsight is a wonderful thing and I can see now that I've always been attracted to women, but my brain chose to ignore it as a way to keep parts of me safe. Growing up in the 1990s in a small village with no visible LGBTQIA+ people in my life meant that I subconsciously shut down my sexuality and tried to fit into what society told me was normal. I'm proud of my younger self for doing her best.

Reading my story again to edit this new edition of the book has been an emotional reminder of all the ways my marriage helped me grow as a person. I'll always be grateful for the love as well as for having someone to lean on for 17 years. Without that I may have fallen down for good, unable to find a way to stand tall on my own.

It felt misplaced to mention this bittersweet conclusion in the main part of my story, but it's also so much more to me than just a footnote in my life. It's a depth of connection to myself that I never saw coming. An ending, a new beginning, a surprise and an inevitability.

RESOURCES

GENERAL MENTAL HEALTH RESOURCES

UK

Mental Health Foundation UK:
www.mentalhealth.org.uk
Mind UK: www.mind.org.uk
Rethink Mental Illness: www.rethink.org
Samaritans: www.samaritans.org, helpline: 116 123
Scottish Association for Mental Health (SAMH):
www.samh.org.uk
Shout: www.giveusashout.org, text 85258
Young Minds: www.youngminds.org.uk

Europe

Mental Health Europe: www.mhe-sme.org
Mental Health Ireland: www.mentalhealthireland.ie

USA

HelpGuide: www.helpguide.org
Mentalhealth.gov: www.mentalhealth.gov
Mental Health America: www.mhanational.org

National Alliance on Mental Illness (NAMI):
www.nami.org
National Institute of Mental Health: www.nimh.nih.gov
Very Well Mind: www.verywellmind.com

Canada
Canadian Mental Health Association: cmha.ca
Crisis Service Canada: www.ementalhealth.ca

Australia and New Zealand
Beyond Blue: www.beyondblue.org.au
Head to Health: headtohealth.gov.au
Health Direct: www.healthdirect.gov.au
Mental Health Australia: mhaustralia.org
Mental Health Foundation of New Zealand:
www.mentalhealth.org.nz
SANE Australia: www.sane.org

ANXIETY-SPECIFIC RESOURCES

In the following websites you can find guidance, support, advice and treatment options.

UK
Anxiety UK: www.anxietyuk.org.uk
No More Panic: www.nomorepanic.co.uk
No panic: www.nopanic.org.uk
Social Anxiety: www.social-anxiety.org.uk

USA
Anxiety and Depression Association of America: www.adaa.org

Canada
Anxiety Canada: www.anxietycanada.com

Australia and New Zealand
Anxiety New Zealand Trust: www.anxiety.org.nz
Black Dog Institute: www.blackdoginstitute.org.au

SUPPORT FOR SUICIDAL THOUGHTS

If you are finding it difficult to cope or know someone who is, and need to be heard without judgment or pressure, you can find information and support from the following:

Crisis Text Line (US, Canada, Ireland, UK): www.crisistextline.org

UK
Campaign Against Living Miserably (CALM): www.thecalmzone.net
PAPYRUS (dedicated to the prevention of young suicide): www.papyrus-uk.org
The Samaritans: www.samaritans.org

USA
American Foundation for Suicide Prevention: afsp.org
National Suicide Prevention Lifeline: suicidepreventionlifeline.org

Canada
Canada Suicide Prevention Crisis Service: www.crisisservicescanada.ca

Australia and New Zealand
Lifeline Australia: www.lifeline.org.au

PODCASTS

A selection of podcasts about depression, mental health, wellbeing and therapy:

Bewildered: Martha Beck and Rowan Mangan
Bryony Gordon's Mad World
Feel Better, Live More: Dr Chatterjee
Happy Place: Fearne Cotton
Let's Talk about CBT: Dr Lucy Maddox
Man Talk: Jamie Day
Mental Health Foundation Podcasts
The One You Feed: Eric Zimmer
People Soup: Ross McIntosh
Psychologists off the Clock: Debbie Sorensen, Diana Hill, Yael Schonrbun
Pulling The Thread: Elise Loehnen
Terrible, Thanks for Asking: Nora Mcireny
Therapy for Black Girls: Joy Hayden Bradford
Therapy Lab: Dr Sheri Jacobson
We Can Do Hard Things: Glennon Doyle

BOOKS

Books About Personal Experiences of Depression
Gordon, Bryony, *Mad Girl* (Headline, 2016)
Haig, Matt, *Reasons to Stay Alive* (Canongate, 2015)
Lawson, Jenny, Furiously *Happy: A funny book about horrible things* (Flatiron, 2015)
Mackie, Bella, *Jog On* (William Collins, 2019)
Reed, Charlotte, *My Path to Happy: Struggles with my mental health and all the wonderful things that happened after* (Andrews McMeel Publishing, 2020)
Sanders, Ali, *When the Bough Breaks* (Trigger, 2019)
Williams, Mark, *Daddy Blues* (Trigger, 2018)
Williams, Terrie M, *Black Pain: It just looks like we're not hurting* (Scribner, 2009)
Wix, Katie, *Delicacy* (Headline, 2021)

Books about Wellbeing, Self-Care or to Inspire
Aiyana, Sheleana, *Becoming the One* (Rider, 2022)
Chatterjee, Dr Rangan, *The Four Pillar Plan* (Penguin, 2017)
Curtis, Scarlett, *It's Not OK to Feel Blue (and Other Lies)* (Penguin, 2020)
Macksey, Charlie, *The Boy, The Mole, The Fox and The Horse* (Ebury, 2019)

Nagoski, Emily, & Nagoski, Amelia, *Burnout*
(Ebury, 2020)
Novogratz, Sukey, & Novogratz, Elizabeth, *Just Sit:
A meditation guidebook for people who know they
should but don't* (Harper Wave, 2017)
Reading, Suzy, *Self-care for Tough Times* (Aster, 2021)
Reading, Suzy, *The Self-care Revolution* (Aster, 2017)
Wax, Ruby, *How to be Human* (Penguin Life, 2018)
Weintraub, Amy, *Yoga for Depression*
(Broadway Books, 2003)

ACKNOWLEDGEMENTS

Thank you to Trigger and Welbeck for giving me a platform to share my story.

Thank you to my agent Jo Bell for finding me and for being the calming voice of reason.

Thank you to Christine, Elli, Emily C, Emily H, Fay, Jo H, Jo L, Kasim, Michelle, Sinead and Sofia.

Thank you to Mum, Dad, Stuart and Colin.

To Claire, Kirsty, Nicola and Jess, thank you for rallying round and getting me up the road.

Finally, thank you to anyone who has ever sent me an email, private message or left a comment on my blog. You reminded me to keep going.

TriggerHub.org is one of the most elite and scientifically proven forms of mental health intervention

Trigger Publishing is the leading independent mental health and wellbeing publisher in the UK and US. Clinical and scientific research conducted by assistant professor Dr Kristin Kosyluk and her highly acclaimed team in the Department of Mental Health Law & Policy at the University of South Florida (USF), as well as complementary research by her peers across the US, has independently verified the power of lived experience as a core component in achieving mental health prosperity. Specifically, the lived experiences contained within our bibliotherapeutic books are intrinsic elements in reducing stigma, making those with poor mental health feel less alone, providing the privacy they need to heal, ensuring they know the essential steps to kick-start their own journeys to recovery, and providing hope and inspiration when they need it most.

Delivered through TriggerHub, our unique online portal and accompanying smartphone app, we make our library of bibliotherapeutic titles and other vital resources accessible to individuals and organizations anywhere, at any time and with complete privacy, a crucial element of recovery. As such, TriggerHub is the primary recommendation across the UK and US for the delivery of lived experiences.

At Trigger Publishing and TriggerHub, we proudly lead the way in making the unseen become seen. We are dedicated to humanizing mental health, breaking stigma and challenging outdated societal values to create real action and impact. Find out more about our world-leading work with lived experience and bibliotherapy via triggerhub.org, or by joining us on:

🐦 @triggerhub_

📘 @triggerhub.org

📷 @triggerhub_